LIFE TOUCHED WITH WONDER

LIFE TOUCHED WITH WONDER

A MESSAGE
of FAMILY

FROM THE EDITORS OF READER'S DIGEST

THE READER'S DIGEST ASSOCIATION, INC.
PLEASANTVILLE, NEW YORK

CONTENTS

LIFE TOUCHED
WITH WONDER

*Men wonder at the height of mountains, the huge waves of the sea, the broad
flow of rivers, the course of the stars—and forget to wonder at themselves.*
— *St. Augustine*

We feel awe when we see a grand landscape or view the majesty of a
starry sky. But there's also wonder in a child's kiss when you're feeling
down, in a friend's unexpected recovery from a frightening illness, in a walk
on a hushed, snowy night. Such moments take us by surprise and lift us
from the mundane and the familiar. Suddenly, inexplicably, we catch a
glimpse of a reality beyond ourselves, and see evidence that there is something beautiful, merciful, loving knit into the fabric of creation — even in
ourselves.

In fact, ordinary people can be the most gifted messengers of wonder.
Their stories offer compelling evidence of the power of the spirit in daily
life. In this new book series we have selected the best of such true-life stories and present them in separate volumes organized around themes.

The stories in *A Message of Family* show us the amazing strength we draw
from our parents, our children, our brothers and sisters—indeed from all
those who occupy that most intimate inner circle of our lives. Their exam-
ples remind us of what's really important, and that we are all vital members
of the family of man.

THE DAY I MET MY MOTHER

BY

FAITH L. MAHANEY

*M*ine was, at times, a solitary childhood. Born in Chungking, China, of missionary parents, I lost my mother at birth. I was two months old when my distraught father sent me to Mother's favorite sister in Morgantown, West Virginia. There I grew up in the house where Mother had spent her childhood.

When Aunt Ruth was at home, I was surrounded by love. But she was our sole breadwinner and worked in an office six days a week. Left with a procession of hired girls, I felt the loneliness of the big, old house.

In the evenings, before Aunt Ruth came home, I often sat on the floor beneath a picture of my mother—a sweet-faced young woman of 20, with dark eyes and black curly hair. Sometimes I talked to the picture, but I could never bear to look at it when I'd been naughty. There was one question always in my mind: *What was my mother like?*

Twenty years passed. I had grown up, married and had a baby, named Lucy for her grandmother—the mother I'd so longed to know.

One spring morning, 18-month-old Lucy and I boarded a train for Morgantown to visit Aunt Ruth. A woman offered me half her seat in

2

the crowded car. I thanked her and busied myself with Lucy, while the woman turned her attention to the landscape speeding by.

After settling my baby in my arms for a nap, I started to talk with the woman. She said she was going to Morgantown to see her daughter and brand-new grandson. "Surely you know my aunt, Ruth Wood," I said. "She had a real estate office in Morgantown for years."

"No," she answered. "I've been away a long time, and that name is not familiar to me."

For several minutes, the woman looked out the window. Then, without turning her head, she began to speak.

"There was a Miss Lucy Wood, a teacher, in Morgantown years ago. She probably left there before you were born. You said the name *Wood*, and, suddenly, I can't stop thinking about her. I haven't thought of her for years, but once I loved her very much. She was my teacher. My parents owned a bakery on Watts Street. They were on the verge of divorce. They fought and quarreled all the time. I had to work very hard at home and in the bakery, too.

"I loved school, though I didn't make good grades. Miss Wood's room was a happy place; it seemed like heaven to me. One day, after my folks had a big fight at breakfast, I came to school late, holding back the tears. Miss Wood kept me after school. I thought she would scold me but, instead, she let me tell her my troubles. She made me feel how much my brothers and sisters, and even my parents, needed me—and from that day on, my life was worth living.

"A few months later, I heard a little girl say, 'Miss Wood's going to marry a missionary and go live in China!' I went home crying. My parents stopped in the middle of a fight to ask me what was wrong, but they could not know how great a light was going out in my life. I couldn't sleep that night.

"The next day, Miss Wood again kept me after school to see what was wrong. When I told her, she looked surprised and tender. 'Please *don't* go way off to China!' I begged.

"'Viola,' she answered, 'I can't give up China. I'm going where my heart calls me, with the man I love. But I'll think of you often, and I'll send you a postcard.'

"I'd never had any mail of my own, so that made me feel better. When I told my mother, she shook her head, saying, 'Don't feel too bad, Viola, if she forgets; she'll have so many folks to write to.'

"Two months later, I got a postcard with a picture of the Yangtzee River, postmarked Chungking, China. 'Are you still making me proud of you, my little brave one?' it asked. If anyone had given me a million dollars, it couldn't have made me more proud.

"Right after that, my parents broke up and we moved away from Morgantown. I raised my five brothers and sisters, married, and raised four children of my own.

"Goodness, we are almost there! I've talked too much. I do hope I haven't bored you."

Then, for the first time, she turned to me and saw the tears in my eyes.

"Would you like to see Lucy Wood's granddaughter?" I asked. My baby was waking from her nap. My heart was singing. The burning question of my childhood had been richly answered. At long last, I knew exactly what my mother had been like.

To forget one's ancestors is to be a brook

without a source, a tree without a root.

CHINESE PROVERB

A MESSAGE OF FAMILY

BY
SHELBY HEARON

*S*everal summers ago, 48 of my kinfolk from ten states converged on San Marcos, Texas, for my parents' golden wedding anniversary. Being with four dozen relatives like this got me to thinking a lot about Family— and most of all, it reminded me that Family is different from nonfamily.

For many of us, Family is out of style. We suffer our parents on infrequent visits. We don't understand our children. We feel safer, better, when we are with our friends and peers.

After all, our Families knew us *when*. Uncle Avery taught me my first word ("No!"); Aunt Katherine gave me my first spanking ("If you don't stop that crying, *I'll* give you something to cry about!"). Besides Uncle Avery and Aunt Katherine, my father had three other sisters and another brother. They all grew up in Marion, Kentucky, in a huge two-story house with five bedrooms, a banister to slide down, a linen closet to hide in, a cedar chest filled with cracked china dolls, and a barn that burned to the ground the summer that I was ten.

We Cousins got free run of the place when we summered there, and we would sit around and listen to the Aunts and Uncles tell stories about what they did when they were young. There was the time Avery almost chopped off three of his sister Louisa's fingers with an ax. Or—in a freak accident—the time that he and Daddy were playing mumble-typeg in the yard and Daddy ended up with a bad knife injury in his head, blood pouring down his face. In the telling of the tale, both men always got down on the floor and argued again the strategies of the game.

If you were part of the Family, a bad word could never be spoken against you. After Uncle Ed married his Divorced Woman, her past was not mentioned again. When Aunt Virginia's husband took to drink, the staunchest teetotalers looked after him, accepting this as a Problem in the Family.

Until that summer in San Marcos, I hadn't seen these Aunts and Uncles for 20 years or more, and yet they seemed unchanged. Aunt Martha, a diminutive psychologist, was still elegant, with curly hair and gorgeous purple-silk blouses. Louisa, the baby girl at 66, still retained, despite years of teaching math in the roughest section of Detroit, the same sweet-little-girl smile I remembered. Katherine, the eldest, the one who had taken me under her wing whenever possible in an effort to shape me up, had at 80 just retired after some 50 years of teaching and of guiding tours to Europe.

The Uncles, too, were the same, only no longer fat. Daddy had lost 30 pounds to be the weight he was when he married. Uncle Ed had spruced himself up for his second wife. And Uncle Avery, my favorite, everyone's favorite, was also thinner for a more somber reason: he was fighting bone cancer.

That was the major difference from the Aunts and Uncles I had known before: mortality had come to their attention. Death was no longer a topic that concerned their parents—it now addressed the Brothers and Sisters directly. Since I had seen them last, their sister Virginia had died, Ed had buried his first wife, and all three remaining

sisters had been widowed. Before the reunion, Avery had written each of us about his cancer. Now taking a female hormone, he was suddenly free of pain and optimistic again. They all joked with him constantly about the hormone; but beneath the surface was knowledge that this might be their, our, last visit with him.

We Cousins, however, were not thinking of eternity. We were all busy trying to make places for ourselves in a world that was not that of our parents. At the same time, we also wanted to figure out who our parents really were. We each knew scraps, based on overheard conversations and early stories about them. We tried to make a whole of it.

We talked about what it had meant to be descended from a grandmother who had borne nine children, buried two and instilled in the rest her drive for learning—back at a time when birth control was not an option—and from an irascible grandfather, who looked like Colonel Sanders and lived to be 94.

At the reunion, as in the Family, we Cousins were the in-between generation. We had grown up on temperance lectures, on the assumption of lifelong monogamy, on education as the first priority, and kinship as the second. Our parents thought we had strayed from their teachings (several of us were divorced), and they could not understand our new expectations. Our children, on the other had, thought our goals for them too rigid and too demanding.

They, the Second Cousins, took to one another immediately. Why not? They had us in common. They swam, got tans, fished, fed corn to the swans. The little ones had their diapers changed; second-graders played slumber party; a four-year-old girl baited a boy cousin's hook.

The Brothers and Sisters took pictures of it all. They grouped us endlessly: by the families we came from and the ones we had made. They could tell, they insisted, who was who by the resemblance. We all looked like them, our parents or our grandparents. This proved, they said, that nothing was lost. It just got passed along.

The golden wedding celebration ended with a banquet at which the Brothers and Sisters reigned at the head table and we all went back for thirds on the roast beef and ham and creamed potatoes. When the groom kissed the bride and they got into an argument about his rendition of the song played at their wedding, when my mother received a nostalgic blowup of their wedding picture and didn't like it any more than she had the first time, when Daddy had his picture taken with the bill—we knew we were home.

We Cousins watched it all. We were the understudies waiting in the wings. We were learning the message of Family, knowing that our turn was next—that each of those at the head table was once a ten-year-old playing mumbletypeg, that each of us who now held our sweetheart's hand under the table would one day be alone. We also learned, perhaps, that in wanting to become something our parents were not, we had lost something they were.

I envisioned my three sisters and myself at some future reunion. It would be like this one. There would be the same things between us: love and old angers, empathy and missed connections. We would tell one another all the old stories about what we had done back then.

At the end, when Charles and Evelyn cut the white-and-yellow wedding cake and we all stood and drank a toast to their anniversary with our iced tea, we wept—for their union, and our own.

"KEEP PEDALING, KAREN!"

BY
CHRISTOPHER DE VINCK

Once I found a pink moth on our front porch. I was perhaps eight years old, and it happened as I stepped out through my front door into the glass-enclosed vestibule, nearly like a greenhouse, where we left our boots in the winter. A moth was desperately trying to find its way off the porch.

Several times I had found a bee or a moth trapped on the porch, and I always caught it and let it go. But I noticed this moth was a color I had never seen before—pink, completely pink. I caught the moth, held it in my hands.

What does a boy do with a pink moth? I found a shoe box, filled it with grass and a soda cap of water and placed my moth in the box.

It died, of course. Things cannot be held too long—they need to be set free. I threw the shoe box, the soda cap and the grass into the garbage can, and I buried the moth in the garden.

Even today, I feel as though I am always being pulled between wanting to hold on to things and wanting to let them go. I remember the afternoon Karen learned how to ride her bicycle alone for the first time.

We began in the early fall, Karen and I. I took off her training wheels, but she insisted I hold on to the handlebar and the seat as we walked down the street.

"I'll just let go for a second, Karen."

"No!" she insisted.

Perhaps Karen will be a lawyer someday or a singer. Perhaps she will make a discovery, give birth to her own daughter. I thought about these things as we wiggled and rattled our way around the block.

It didn't take her long to understand how to turn the pedals with her feet. As I held on to the bicycle, Karen's head and dark hair were just to the right of my cheek.

After a few weeks, Karen was comfortable enough with my letting the handlebar go, but I still had to hold on to the rear of the seat.

"Don't let go, Daddy."

Halloween. Thanksgiving. The leaves disappeared. We spent less and less time practicing. Wind. Cold. Winter. I hung Karen's bicycle on a nail in the garage.

Christmas. Among Karen's favorite gifts that year were five pieces of soap in the shape of little shells, which her mother had bought.

New Year's Eve. Snow. High fuel bills. And then a sudden warm spell.

"Roe," I said to my wife as we woke up, "do you hear that bird singing? It's a cardinal." Roe and I listened. The children were downstairs watching television.

After breakfast, I found Karen in the garage trying to unhook her bicycle. I walked into the garage and lifted the bike off the nail.

She hopped on, and I pushed her across the crushed stones of our driveway to the street. I gave her a slight shove. "Let go, Daddy!" and Karen simply wobbled, shook, laughed and pedaled off as I stood alone watching her spin those wheels against the blacktop.

Einstein spoke about time, about the speed of light and objects moving toward and away from each other. I wanted to run to Karen,

hold the seat of her bicycle, hold on to her handlebar, have her dark hair brush against my cheek. Instead I kept shouting, "Keep pedaling, Karen! Keep pedaling!" And then I applauded.

There is no use holding on to the pink moth, or your daughter. They will do just fine on their own. Just set them free.

Keep pedaling, Karen. Keep pedaling.

He who has daughters is always a shepherd.

SPANISH PROVERB

"JUST BE READY!"

BY

ANNETTA HEREFORD BRIDGES

On Wednesday she first noticed the feeling—a restless something that nagged like a forgotten name. The big man had seemed fretful, and she had suggested a checkup. "Haven't got the time," he grunted. "Lab classes today."

That night she had a vivid dream. She was sixteen again, watching in awe as the bronze giant her brother had brought home from college tossed 200-pound bales of hay into the barn loft. Then, suddenly, she looked down to see the same body lying on the floor at her feet.

She sat up, heart thumping. But the big man beside her was sleeping peacefully.

On Friday, at her insistence, the man was examined, and came home with a pleased smile on his face. "See?" he said. "I told you I was fine!" But during the night a voice wakened her: *"Be ready . . . just be ready."*

The man beside her stirred. *"Now* what's wrong?"

"Nothing," she whispered.

On Saturday she hid her feelings all day in a frenzy of housework, and on Sunday she suggested the man stay in bed a while. He surprised her by agreeing, then read the paper, then paced the floor.

That night she counted the hours and dozed fitfully. Monday she moved vaguely through the day, waiting for something definable, watching for something definite. Another night. Lightheaded now from lack of sleep.

Tuesday dawned clear and beautiful. The calendar said February 3, but the temperature was a mild 55, and on the hill behind the Texas ranch house spring already pushed green fingers through the dry grass. Even when the five young adults they had created were not around, there was plenty to do: cattle to feed, the garden to tend, the house closets to finish. And always their teaching chores. Last night they had set the alarm early because the man had a field trip scheduled today for his physics classes.

Six o'clock. *Please stay home,* she said silently. But what reason could she give? She pulled on her clothes and went through the hall toward the kitchen. Then she heard it—an oddly soft sound. And even before she turned, she knew, *"Be ready!"*

At the end of the hall, the big man lay crumpled in a curve on his right side. His feet were in the bedroom, his head was wedged against the bathroom doorframe, his arms were twisted under the hard-muscled, 260-pound body. She raced to his side, but already his face was darkening, and his eyes were rolled back.

Swiftly, fingers to the wrist. *No pulse.* She bent her face close to his. *No breath.*

Oh, dear God!

The head was all wrong; the neck bent too far to allow him air. She clawed at his arms, legs, pulled at his shoulders, hoping to roll the body, straighten the neck. On her knees, she tugged with all her strength. The head was still wedged. She grabbed his feet, catching both under her arms, and pulled toward the open bedroom door. One inch, two. The head rolled, the neck straightened. She pulled at the right arm again, and the shoulder moved slightly to the right, as the body's left side settled toward the floor.

The man's face was black now, the eyes dilated. She laid her left hand over her right on the wide chest, and pushed down hard. Up. Down. Her

110 pounds against his 260. She bent her elbows, released the pressure. Again. Up and down.

Bits and pieces of their lives seemed to float away from the body. *The navy uniform. The babies they'd buried. The giant sons in football games. The lovely talented daughters. All five in college at once.* Down, two, three, four. Was she going too fast? She watched the procedure from afar now, a spectator viewing actions in slow motion: 15, 16; up, down.

All five children are about through school, now, and maybe we can . . . no. Not if . . . 20, 25 . . . *The grandbabies. Such love* . . . 30, 35. . . . He had worked so hard for so long. He had wished for a secondhand wagon this summer, to travel . . . 45, 50, 55. . . . *So many things. Like see Alaska.*

Sixty, 65, 70, 80. Her arms: they weren't going to make it. . . . *Please, God . . . 85, 86, 87. Squish!* A gurgle!

Oh, God, I'm ready!

A gasp, then the body heaved, and she pumped harder, harder. The heart fluttered, caught, fluttered again. Still she pumped, arms numb, and the big arms started to flail.

The chest rose, throwing her against the wall, as the man gasped and struggled for air. The arms waved, the legs bucked. Something crashed into the back of her head. He had kicked the louvered doors of the water-heater closet from their tracks. Knocking the door aside, she whirled to pull the feet from under the heater burner, and the man raised himself up on an elbow, mouth open.

A doctor. An ambulance. The phone. Thank God, the extension was just above her head. "Breathe!" she screamed at the man. "Breathe!"

The run of miracles began. For the first time ever, on an eight-party line, she got the operator on one try. "Hurry! An ambulance!" she shouted. The driver answered—incredible!—after one ring. She yelled directions. "And hurry! *Please* hurry!" But it was at least 20 miles.

More gurgles. But the face was darkening again. She went back to pumping with both hands. The heart fluttered and stopped, fluttered and caught. When the beat had steadied a bit, she ran across the bedroom to open a window. Cold air poured in, and the man opened his mouth and took great gulps. His face turned to gray, to red.

Long ragged breaths, then, and finally the strength to gasp for water. She reached a glass on the lavatory through the doorway, gave him a pill the doctor had given him on Friday for "shortness of breath."

Help him breathe, Lord, help him. She propped him against the door and dialed the doctor. Another miracle: she caught him, asked him to meet them at the hospital. Then an eternity until the ambulance came, oxygen was administered, and the long trip to the hospital began.

Through the wide doors of Emergency. Explanations to doctors, nurses, lab technicians. Then blood samples, X rays, electrocardiograms. The man breathed erratically, raggedly, and they took him up to the intensive cardiac-care unit, with monitor of pulse and pressure. And no visitors, no matter who.

The woman kept vigil outside the door, near the nursing station. Once, grabbing a passing nurse, she learned the man was "still breathing comfortably." The slow hours ticked by. Calls to the children were put through—to Mississippi, to Alaska, to three different universities in Texas. "No, don't come yet," she told them, knowing they'd come anyway. "I'll let you know."

One, two, and four o'clock, and through the night. At dawn—splendid and glorious—the man was still alive. They let her see him for five minutes. No talk, but she watched as the lungs drew their ragged breaths, as oxygen gave him life.

The cardiac specialist finally arrived. He shot a needle into a vein, drew blood, did a quick gasses test. "There's no oxygen in his blood! Up that supply! Get that mask on tighter and keep it there!"

A stethoscope probed the massive chest. As the doctor listened, he asked the woman blunt questions. "How long was he not breathing? Skin gray or black? Wet or dry? Fingernails? Eyes?" More listening, then he straightened slowly. "Pulmonary emboli. Multiple," he said. He shook his head. "*More* than multiple."

The cardiologist ordered a computer lung scan. To radiology. An injection of radioactive technetium, split-second timing, plotting by the scanner. Then back to the heart monitor. She read the answer in the cardiac crew's white faces, in the speed with which they pumped anticoagulants into the body.

"A *very* massive pulmonary embolic phenomenon," dictates the cardiologist. The nurses scribble, the men confer. Through the door, the woman strains to see. Finally, the cardiologist comes out; the woman catches him by the sleeve. "Please," she said. "The scan. Can I see it?"

"I don't think you ought to." He looked at her hard, then said gently, "You did bring him back, didn't you? I'll arrange it. Go on down."

The radiologist held the pictures a while, explaining, preparing her. Looking, the woman regretted her request. Instead of two white ovals of lungs, she saw images of two lopsided pieces of Swiss cheese furrowed and chewed into fragments by six black wells of blood clots.

"I've never seen anything like it," said the radiologist. "I understand you saved his life. Are you a nurse?"

"No. A teacher."

"I just don't see how he made it to the hospital. Or how he can poss—"

"He will *live!*" she told the man fiercely, and fled.

Another night, another dawn. Against all odds, the man still breathed. A change came the third day. The racing pulse, nudging 140, gradually slowed to 120, 100, 90. The woman breathed her gratitude, and allowed herself some questions. Why had this happened to a non-smoking, non-drinking, active man? Was it a common thing? Could it have been prevented? She cornered the cardiologist.

"Prevent cardiac arrest from pulmonary emboli? Sometimes. But people like this are walking around everyday, carrying clots ready to kill them. If only they would cut out the salts, the fats, the sweets. If only they would exercise!"

"But he *did* exercise! Every day."

"Maybe that will save him." The cardiologist paused. "There's been something of a miracle here."

"I know," she said.

Ten days later, a five-minute visit per hour. More days, and to the progressive unit and later to a private room. Then a possibility of home.

Home: the big brick ranch they had built themselves; a herd of black Angus grazing; a shed bursting with its crop of hay. The sons and daughters had come, of course—to return to the man some of the strength he had given them for thirty years. His colleagues came and went. And his students.

His wife? I, too, survived, strengthened by the known, sustained by the unknown.

The big man, by an uncommon clutch of miracles, is alive. We are following the doctors' don't's: Don't cross the legs. Don't fail to wear the support hose. Don't forget the daily anticoagulant. Don't stay too long in one position, or forget to exercise or neglect the diet.

Do's? Do resume normal living. Do be grateful you're alive. Do know you're one of the lucky ones.

We've added to a "do" of our own: Do know this experience has a purpose. It points to work yet to be done and promises to keep.

Just be ready, the voice had said.

We're ready, this man and I. Ready for anything.

OUTSIDE LOOKING IN

BY

MARY E. POTTER

I step out the back door and the blackness of night engulfs me. There is no moon to light my way to the clothesline and my forgotten wash. I'm piloted by the memory of a thousand trips along the familiar path: now up two flagstone steps, now past the giant pine whose branches overhang our cottage.

Past the corner of the woodshed, my outstretched hands become my scouts, groping for the lines, fumbling with the pins. Soon my arms are heaped with night-damp pants and shirts that have danced all day to the wind's compelling tunes.

The trip back is easier. As soon as I round the shed, the lights of the house guide me—great squares of amber light suspended in the darkness. The moment my gaze penetrates the glass, I become suspended too.

Everything inside the house appears transformed. The cherry-stained kitchen cabinets look warmer, richer; the shelves of mixing bowls, crocks and casseroles, the rows of spices and jars and bottles, are homier. Even the pine wall behind the stove, so utilitarian with hanging pots, glows with a new personality.

The clothes still weighing down my arms, I back up farther into the yard. From here I can see the living room. John's head is bent over a spelling book, his hair golden in the lamplight, his face set with a frown of concentration. Robert kneels by the sofa, pushing a wheeled Lego contraption along the cliff-edge of the cushion. The corner of a newspaper flaps into sight and disappears as Richard's invisible hands turn the pages. I picture his absorbed face, studious-looking in new reading glasses.

Colored as they are with a rich topaz light, these ordinary scenes now seem imbued with vibrancy and charm, which flow not so much from the lamps as from the feelings of warmth and peace they inspire. For a split second I am a stranger peeking into a home I have never seen before.

I ask myself, What if I really became a stranger? What if I could never get back into these rooms? What if I could never again touch John's springy hair or see Robert's guileless smile?

Deep inside me, a door opens—that barrier we set up to guard our secret selves—and without conditions I let my family in. All the annoyances that families are prone to, all the kinks and stumbling blocks in our relationships, all the difficulties of living together in harmony become trivial—overwhelmed by the simple fact that we love one another.

Moments like this don't occur every day, and maybe that's the way it should be. It would be exhausting to live our lives weighed down by such intensity of feeling. But the memory sustains me, just as the smell of fresh air clings to the clothes in my arms. Tomorrow morning when I slip them on, my armor against the world, the lingering fragrance will remind me that they have danced in the darkness, under the pines, on the edge of a deep, golden light.

MY UNCLE AND ME

BY
PAT JORDAN

My Uncle Ben Diamond was a draftsman, and it was the perfect job for him. He had a clear, logical mind and an esthetic sense to go along with his devotion to detail. He dressed in a preppy way—navy blazer, gray flannel slacks—and his gestures were mesmerizing. A courtly man, he seemed to move a beat or two slower than others.

When I was a boy in Fairfield, Connecticut, I would walk to his place for breakfast every morning. I left early, before my parents began their daily argument. My father was a gambler, and life in our house was at the mercy of his dark moods. So I'd escape to my uncle's childless apartment, which was always as quiet as a church.

I would sit at the dining-room table, surrounded by Aunt Ada's knickknacks and little boxes of violets, while Uncle Ben made our breakfast. (Aunt Ada always slept late, it seemed.) It was an elaborate ritual, and always the same—orange juice, two pieces of buttered toast, one soft-boiled egg and a cup of coffee (mine mostly milk). It was certainly not the usual breakfast for a child, but Uncle Ben made it sound like a king's feast.

He explained how he squeezed the oranges by hand in a cut-glass juicer, never grinding them too hard or there'd be too much pulp in the juice. The toast had to be a perfect shade of tan, he'd say, holding out a slice in the doorway for me to see. Then he'd lay a pat of warm butter on top, let it melt and spread it evenly over the toast. The egg was cooked for exactly three minutes and brought to me in an egg cup. He showed me how to tap around the shell's circumference with the side of my spoon to take the top half off.

Uncle Ben had a way of singing the praises of the most mundane thing so that it became something of wonder to a child.

While we ate, Uncle Ben read the Major League baseball scores from the newspaper, out loud. We were Yankee fans because the Yankees had many Italian-Americans like us: Raschi, Berra, Rizzuto, Crosetti. And, of course, Joltin' Joe DiMaggio. I clapped my hands softly at his mention of their successes and dreamed of being a part of them someday.

After breakfast I helped wash and dry the dishes. When we finished, he'd take a tiny porcelain Buddha out of Aunt Ada's glass breakfront and let me rub its belly for good luck. Then we'd go play catch in his narrow driveway.

He'd get down stiffly into his catcher's crouch, pinching the knees of each pant leg, laying a piece of folded cloth on the pavement as a plate. Then I'd pitch to him. We made believe I faced the mighty Yankees. After each pitch, he would bounce out of his crouch and fire the ball back. "Atta boy, Paddy!" he'd say. "You got him!"

He was always tough on me, until I got behind in the count on Joltin' Joe and he saw my face flush with panic. Then he'd give me a break on a pitch even I knew was off the plate. "Strike three!" he'd call, and fire the ball back so hard it stung my hand. I always pitched a perfect game with Uncle Ben.

Like many childless adults, he didn't have to feign having fun with a child. He really did! Adults with their neuroses and duplicities made him nervous. Children in their innocence calmed him, which was why he jumped at the opportunity to be our town's Little League baseball coach when it was offered to him.

The job came open every two years or so, because the coach was usually the father of one of the players. He'd coach until his son graduated from Little League, then quit. It was assumed that Uncle Ben would coach for the two years I was eligible to play and then quit. But 20 years later, after I married and had children of my own, he was still our Little League coach.

Uncle Ben was harder on me than he was on the other players. We both knew this was a ruse to hide his obvious affection. On the field he called me "Jordan," not "Paddy," and he made me carry the heavy canvas bat bag from his car. At batting practice he grunted a little harder when he threw me his fastball, and he never told me when his curve was coming, as he did for others.

I was the team's star pitcher, and no matter how hard he tried, my uncle could never really hide his pleasure when I was on the mound. It would be the final inning of a one-run game, with a runner on third base and two outs. He would pace back and forth, yelling encouragement. "Come on, Paddy! You can do it!" (I wasn't Jordan then.) I would get two strikes on the batter and, before I delivered, I'd give my uncle a wink and get strike three. He would charge out to shake my hand.

Uncle Ben ran constant herd on us to act like men. I remember the one time he ever really spoke harshly to me. It was before a game I was not scheduled to pitch. I was fooling around, showing off for the benefit of some 12-year-old girls who had come to flirt. I put my cap on backward, and my shoes were unlaced in a deliberately sloppy manner to elicit laughter. My uncle barked at me, "Fix your hat and shoes, Jordan! Look like a ballplayer!"

I sulked for the entire game. I felt humiliated. Afterward, as my uncle drove home, I sat in glum silence. He tried to explain why he had snapped at me over such an inconsequential matter.

"It's important how you look, Paddy," he said. "Details, like wearing your uniform just so, add up. They count. If you do all the little things right, then when the big things come it'll be easier to handle them. And, sometimes, the little things are all you have in life. You can take great satisfaction in those details."

As a child of 12, I only vaguely understood what my uncle was talking about. I understand now, of course. He was talking about pride in oneself. He was talking about his own life, really.

People came from all over the state to see me pitch that year. In the six games that I pitched, I threw four no-hitters and two one-hitters. And our team also won when I wasn't pitching.

My uncle's secret to success was to know the limits of his boys and never push them beyond those limits. He kept things simple and orderly. Other managers overextended their players by concocting elaborate plays that always seemed to backfire and humiliate the boys in front of their parents. Those managers wanted to show the fans how much *they* knew. My uncle always managed in a way that kept the attention on us, not him.

We were a heavy favorite to win the state championship on our way to the Little League World Series at Williamsport, Pennsylvania. But we lost our final game and were eliminated. I pitched a one-hitter that day before 3,000 fans. But I threw wildly on a bunt attempt early in the game, which let in what proved to be the only run. After the game, we were presented trophies at home plate. When my name was announced, the crowd rose and gave me a standing ovation. My uncle walked out to the plate with his arm around my shoulder. I began to cry. He was crying too.

We drifted apart as I became a teenager. He still saw me as a child. I began to see my uncle as lovable, but eccentric. He seemed fussy and enmeshed in the myriad details he felt were so important. His interests seemed trivial.

When I was 18, I signed a $35,000 bonus contract with the Milwaukee Braves and went away to the minor leagues. After three years of diminishing success, I was released by the farm club. I went home, depressed and confused by this first failure of my life.

My bride and I were living, temporarily, at my parents' house near the ball park where I had had so many youthful successes. My parents had offered us the use of their house until, as my mother put it, "you get back on your feet."

But I couldn't get back on my feet. I spent most of each day lying on the bed in my old room, staring straight ahead. The sun came in through the window, illuminating in a dusty haze the mementos of my career arranged on the bureau. Bronzed trophies from Little League, scuffed baseballs from notable high-school successes. What had gone wrong?

I stared at those mementos for long hours, not really seeing them, but rather lost in a kind of lassitude that made even the simplest tasks—dressing, reading the newspaper, going down to dinner, talking with my wife—seem superfluous.

Downstairs in the kitchen, I could hear whispering voices.

"What's wrong with him?" my mother said.

"I don't know," my wife answered, sobbing softly.

Then my uncle called one day. "Paddy, it's me, Uncle Ben," he said, as if I could ever forget his voice. "Why don't you come over tomorrow for breakfast?"

Happiness depends

upon ourselves.

ARISTOTLE

"I'll see," I said. I had no intention of going, but my mother insisted. "It will hurt him terribly if you don't."

It was just the way it had been when I was a child. The orange juice. The perfect toast. Uncle Ben showed it to me through the doorway before he buttered it. "See," he said. "Tan." He wasn't trying to humor me; he was just transporting me back to that simpler time of my childhood.

After we did the dishes, he smiled and said, "I've got something for you." He went into the dining room and opened Aunt Ada's breakfront. Returning with her Buddha, he said, "Remember this, Paddy?"

I smiled. He held it out to me. I rubbed its belly for luck.

Maybe it was the Buddha. Maybe it was just seeing my uncle still take such pleasure in the little details of his life. But I was all right after that. It dawned on me that my life, far from being over, was just beginning. I had a wife. I was 22 years old, and there were so many things out there for me to do. I went back to college. Had children. Taught school. Became a writer. Filled my life with a host of things that give me pleasure.

Then, suddenly, my uncle was gone. I was stunned. I thought he'd always be there. And in a way he is.

I think a lot about my uncle these days, especially when I begin to feel sorry for myself. He never allowed himself to indulge in self-pity, even in the face of the one great disappointment of his life—not having a child of his own.

For Uncle Ben, happiness was never a given. It was worked at, created. He was a master at finding joy in life's details. He showed me how to take delight in small, everyday pleasures. Like perfect, buttered toast.

SISTERS THREE

BY

FAITH ANDREWS BEDFORD

When Mother died, Dad gave up the summer house. "Come and take what you want, girls," he had said to us—and we did.

I chose the tall secretary where Mother sat so often writing letters by a sunny window. Beth chose a painting of the summer house. Ellen picked a statue of horses, for she and Mother had shared a love of riding. Then we put drawers full of old letters, slides and faded photos—the collective memory of a family—into a dozen boxes, and each of us chose four.

Later I sat on the top step of my porch and opened a box marked "albums." Here were photographs of my father, resplendent in his Navy uniform, and one of my mother leaning against their first car. As I leafed through the pages, the family grew—we bought our first house, the cars got bigger. Then, on the last page, there was a picture of us in our matching "sister dresses."

I could almost feel the starched ruffles and hear the rustle of the crinolines that were needed to keep the skirts full. I remembered Mother's delight when she found these outfits at the children's shop in the village. There was one in my size and one for Ellen, but no size four for Beth. We were so excited when the shopkeeper told us she could order a dress for Beth that would come in time for Easter.

When the box arrived we gathered around Mother as she lifted out the dresses. They were made of clouds of white organdy with blue flocked dots. The skirts and collars were trimmed with tiny blue bows. "To match your eyes," Mother said.

We were allowed to try them on just once so we could have a "fashion show" for Father that evening. As we twirled into the dining room in our finery, he burst into applause. We daintily grasped the ruffled skirts and executed our best curtsies.

As I looked at the photograph, I could recall the warmth of the pale spring sunshine on our faces on Easter Sunday. We must have resisted putting on coats to go to church. They surely would have crushed our dresses—and besides, how then could anyone have seen how beautifully we matched?

In time, I handed my dress down to Ellen and she handed hers down to Beth. But those dotted swiss creations were only the beginning of a long parade of matching sister outfits. I remember the year of the blue calicoes and the year we all had yellow jumpers. Even Father got into the spirit when he came back from a business trip to Arizona with Mexican dresses for each of his girls—including Mother.

Those wonderful white dresses, with rows of bright ribbons edging the wide collars and hems, had skirts that were cut in a complete circle. Father put Ravel's "Bolero" on the record player and we spun madly about the living room, our beribboned skirts fluttering like butterflies. At last we crashed, giggling, into a heap. Dad sat in his armchair and grinned his "that's-my-girls" smile.

I remember these first sister dresses so clearly that I'm surprised I can't remember the last ones. Maybe Mother knew we were outgrowing the idea. I think she saw how different we were becoming and just stopped buying us matching dresses.

By the time we were adults, our lives were on three very distinct tracks. Mother would shake her head in bewilderment and say to Father, "How did we get three daughters so different?" He would merely smile.

We knew Christmas would be bittersweet that first year without Mother. For as long as I can remember, Dad had always given Mother a beautiful nightgown at Christmas—long and silky with plenty of lace. The tree sparkled, but there was no big box from "Sweet Dreams" beneath it. Though we put on happy faces for the sake of our children, the little touches that Mother always added were missing.

Suddenly Ellen drew out from behind the tree three identical white packages. On the lids, written in Dad's bold hand, were the words "From the Nightie Gnome." We opened the presents, revealing three identical red flannel nightshirts.

Whooping with delight, we pulled them from the tissue paper and ran down the hall to put them on. When we came back to show off our sister nighties, Dad had put "Bolero" on the stereo. We joined hands and did an impromptu dance. As the music grew louder, we twirled around faster and faster, ignoring the widening eyes of our disbelieving husbands and the gaping mouths of our children.

I smile now at the sight we must have made: Three grown women dressed in red flannel nighties whirling madly through a jumble of empty boxes and wrapping paper. When the music ended in a clash of cymbals, we crashed, giggling, into a heap.

Our husbands shook their heads in wonder. The younger children nearly keeled over with embarrassment while the older ones held their sides with laughter. Dad just cracked his "that's-my-girls" grin.

Mother never realized what a tradition she'd started.

The family fireside is the best of schools.

ARNOLD H. GLASOW

"I'M NOT LETTING YOU GO, DAD!"

BY

WILLIAM M. HENDRYX

Rodolfo "Rudy" Ruiz couldn't wait to get out on the water. After a hectic workweek, the 44-year-old pharmaceutical salesman was eager to go fishing with his son, John David, 14, and his old buddy, John Prodajko. So hours before daybreak on July 25, 1992, Rudy was checking out his four-man inflatable boat, electric trolling motor and 12-volt battery. Meanwhile, John David gleefully dug for worms outside their San Antonio home.

It was almost noon before Prodajko, running late, arrived. A tall, trim Army sergeant on leave from Fort Bliss in El Paso, Prodajko, 29, had heard that small-mouth bass were plentiful on the Blanco River, 50 miles north, and had invited the Ruizes to fish with him there.

The three loaded their gear and drove to a tackle shop. Rudy sent his son off to pick out a couple of lures, and the boy returned with a handful. "Just a minute," Rudy said, smiling. "I said a couple, not a half-dozen!" He put his arm around John David's shoulder. "You know, Son," he added playfully, "I sure love you, but I don't need you."

It was a running joke between them. Several weeks earlier, Rudy had come home to find his wife, Diana, in bed with a bad headache and upset that sons John David and Trey, 17, had avoided their chores. Rudy lectured the boys about how important Diana was to him. He reminded them how she had nursed him through two heart attacks in recent years. Then he added quietly, "I love you boys, too, but I don't need you—not the way I need your mother."

For the next few days, John David wasn't himself. When Rudy asked him what was wrong, John David admitted he felt hurt by Rudy's remark. Father and son talked it over, and the cheerful boy soon turned the incident into a joke.

About four p.m. the fishermen arrived at Bart's Crossing, a low-water area downstream from the town of Blanco. Heavy rains a week earlier had made the river run deeper than normal; still the water looked relatively calm. Rudy had forgotten the rods used for mounting the motor, but he ingeniously rigged a makeshift device by lacing a heavy automobile tow rope through the big eyelets across the back of the boat. They loaded the craft with the battery and tackle and waded into the water. John David positioned himself in the nose, John Prodajko sat in the middle, and Rudy took the helm. Finally they were under way.

By early evening they'd had only one good nibble, and their enthusiasm was waning. Then, about 7:30, John David whooped, "I've got one!" and reeled in a good-sized catfish.

"Nice catch, son!" Rudy said proudly. Then, looking downstream, he saw they were nearing a low-water road crossing, a shallow spot where a concrete bridge was submerged under a foot of water. They'd crossed similar sites that afternoon. The water normally runs beneath the bridge through a five-foot-wide rectangular concrete drainage chute that spans the 12-foot-wide bridge. Following heavy rains, however, the

chutes are unable to handle the increased flow, and the surplus simply runs over the top. The surface looked peaceful to the fishermen.

As they approached the crossing, the three planned to step onto the bridge and carry the boat over it. Rudy was about to stand up and reach for the bridge when the craft lurched violently and the right-rear corner disappeared beneath his feet. Somehow, the water had literally snatched the boat from beneath them. John David, weighing only 103 pounds, was tossed onto the bridge surface, and Prodajko was pinned against the bridge by the rush of river water. Meanwhile, Rudy, flailing about in the six-foot-deep water, was being sucked into the drainage chute with incredible force. The water funneling through the chute created a violent whirlpool, pulling Rudy's legs and half of the boat inside.

Rudy grabbed the edge of the bridge, the water lapping at his chin, and tried to lift himself onto the solid surface. He couldn't move. He was unaware that his left leg had become entangled in the thick yellow tow rope he had used to secure the tolling motor. The weight of the boat and motor was like an anchor, pulling his lower body underneath the bridge while he fought to keep his head above the surface. Complicating matters, the other half of the boat had folded behind Rudy's back with a large tackle box wedged in between, pounding against his head and shoulders.

Where's John David? Rudy wondered suddenly, straining to hold on to the mossy concrete. He looked up and saw the boy, apparently dazed, standing in the water flowing over the bridge. "Grab hold of me!" Rudy cried out.

John David, his face contorted with fear, knelt on the bridge and slipped his right arm beneath his father's, then grabbed the back of Rudy's wet T-shirt with his left hand. Together he and Rudy heaved with all their strength, but it was no use. "Uncle John!" John David called to Prodajko. "Come help my dad!"

Let the burden be never so heavy, love makes it light.

ROBERT BURTON

Prodajko, however, was waging his own battle for survival. As the river's swift current pressed him against the side of the bridge, the powerful undertow pulled relentlessly at his legs. Clawing at the slippery surface, Prodajko turned and saw Rudy in a desperate situation only a few feet to his left. John David's plea for help echoed through his ears. Terror showed on the boy's face. "I'm trying!" Prodajko shouted. "But I have to get myself out first."

For more than six minutes John David held on to his father while Prodajko struggled out of the river. Finally, he rolled his body onto the bridge surface, scrambled to his feet and rushed to John David's side.

"I'm caught!" Rudy yelled. "Something's around my leg!"

Prodajko and John David pulled with all their might, but Rudy's short, stocky body didn't budge. "Oh, my leg!" Rudy cried painfully with each tug. John David kept asking him, "Are you okay, Dad? How's your heart?"

Just then, Prodajko glanced up the road and saw a pickup truck slowing to a stop. When the driver, Tiffani Walker, 23, stuck her head out the window, Prodajko yelled, "Can you get some help?"

"I'm on my way!" Tiffani shouted back. She raced up the winding, bumpy road to her home, half a mile away. Her parents were visiting, and Tiffani was sure her father would know what to do. As she drove, she gave instructions to her two passengers, her sister, Taffi, 16, and a friend. "As soon as we get home, call 911!"

Three minutes later she stopped in front of her house. As the two girls ran inside, Tiffani yelled to her father, Rex Walker, 53, "There's a man being sucked under the bridge! We've got to get him out!" Rex quickly jumped into his daughter's truck, and the two headed back toward the crossing.

Moments after Tiffani had gone for help, it occurred to Rudy that he was probably being held down by the small-gauge rope that encircled the boat. The rope's constant pull was causing extreme pain in his left leg, hip and lower back. The leg was also going numb from lack of circulation. "Try to cut the rope!" he yelled. "I can't hang on much longer!"

Prodajko managed to free the tackle box that was wedged behind Rudy's neck. Quickly John David rifled through the box and found Prodajko's filleting knife. Unfortunately, it had not been sharpened since its last use, but it would have to do.

The boy stretched as far as he could, reached into the water and, after several attempts, found the rope—sawing at it with the dull blade until it finally snapped. Nothing happened. Instantly, Rudy knew they had severed the wrong rope and that it was the thick tow line that trapped him. "Try cutting the other rope!" said Rudy, his hopes, and his grip, eroding. "Hurry!"

While Prodajko held fast to Rudy, John David extended his arms and the slender-bladed knife as far beneath himself and the bridge as possible. He found his father's leg, then ran his hand down it until he felt the thick rope. He slid the knife a few inches away from where the rope was binding his father and began sawing. But the dull blade didn't even make a dent in the tough nylon. After switching places with John David, Prodajko had no better luck.

Rudy's spirits sagged. His only other hope was to let the water take him through the drain and out the other end, but he wondered what kind of shape he'd be in when—and if—he emerged. He was attached to the raft, and his chances of filtering through one of these 12-foot tunnels—often filled with limbs and debris following a storm—seemed slim. Still, he couldn't continue much longer, and he knew that John David and Prodajko couldn't either. He could feel it in their slackening grips, see it in their panicked faces: everyone was growing weary.

Rudy made his decision. "You've got to let me go," he said softly to John David, avoiding his eyes. "Otherwise I might pull you in with me."

"No, Dad, no!" screamed John David. "I'm not letting you go!" The horrifying memory of his father's first heart attack—almost three years ago to the day—raced though the boy's mind. If it hadn't been for his mother's hospital background, his father might have died of the massive coronary. Recalling the scene at the hospital when he first saw Rudy's body laced with intravenous tubing, John David lifted his eyes to the darkening sky. "Please, Jesus!" he yelled. "Don't let this happen!"

Struck by his son's plea for divine help, Rudy felt a calm settle over him. He couldn't bear the thought of scarring John David for life by letting him see his father drown. Looking directly into John David's eyes, he said quietly, "Okay son, let's pray."

Gently, John David placed his head next to his father's, and each prayed silently for several seconds. Rudy sought as yet unfound strength to hold on for his son's sake. John David asked how he could be expected to live without his father. When they finished, they stared at one another without speaking, their strength renewed.

Moments later, they heard Tiffani's pickup truck slide to a stop on the gravel road. "Can you help my dad?" John David screamed as Rex Walker approached.

"I don't know!" Rex called. Quickly he removed his sneakers and waded onto the bridge. As Rex stared into the murky water, he saw something no one else had noticed in the fading light: on each side of Rudy, submerged under two and a half feet of water, was a six-inch-thick concrete wall jutting three feet upstream from the mouth of the drain. If he could brace himself behind one of those walls, Rex thought, he should be able to free the man's leg without getting sucked in himself.

Rex took the filleting knife from John Prodajko and stepped cautiously into the river.

"Don't get in!" Rudy and John David yelled simultaneously.

"It's okay," Rex said, keeping one hand on the bridge as he waded deeper and deeper into the water. "I know what I'm doing." Setting his feet firmly beside the submerged wall, he bent over as far as possible. He could hear the boy mumbling continuously in his father's ear: "It's gonna be okay, Dad. It's gonna be okay."

Forced to use his left hand, the right-handed Walker reached into the drain and found Rudy's entangled leg. Working blindly, he slipped the filleting knife beneath the rope and awkwardly began sawing. But he quickly realized the blade was too dull.

Suddenly remembering his faithful pocketknife, Rex straightened his back and handed the worthless filleting knife to Prodajko. Then he fished the pocketknife from his pants. Though it was smaller, he always kept it sharp. "Maybe this old thing will do," he said.

Once more he steadied himself against the wall and went back to work. Now the size of the blade made the task harder. With his nose just above the water, Rex pushed and pulled, pushed and pulled. Finally he felt the first of the three strands pop loose, then the second. His hand slipped as Rudy's leg suddenly jerked, but Rex found the groove he'd cut and began again. At last, the final strand broke free.

Rudy felt the pressure release instantly. "Thank you, Lord!" he whispered. Rex grabbed Rudy's leg, helping John David and Prodajko hoist Rudy onto the bridge. The raft disappeared at the same moment. It

Courage is a kind of salvation.

PLATO

should have come out the other side within seconds, but it became lodged inside the chute.

His leg weak and tingling, Rudy sat in the middle of the bridge and rubbed the spot where the rope had bound him. John David put his arms round his father's neck and squeezed tightly, crying, "You're gonna be all right, Daddy!"

Moments later, the Blanco Volunteer Ambulance Corps pulled up and raced to Rudy's side. After checking his vital signs, they heard a loud *swoosh* and saw the inflatable boat come shooting out the other end of the drainage ditch. It had been hung up for several minutes and was all but destroyed.

John David walked over to Rex, put his arms around the stranger's waist and said, "Thank you for saving my daddy's life."

"Just glad I could do it," said Rex quietly, patting the boy's shoulder.

The ambulance crew took Rudy and the others to the emergency medical station and gave them dry clothes. As Rudy sat back enjoying a cup of coffee, John David couldn't resist the opportunity of a lifetime. "Dad," he said with an impish smile, "do you think you need me now?"

On this day, Rudy Ruiz knew he needed his son as never before. He pulled the boy close to him. "Yes, John David," he said. "And I love you, too."

Today Rudy says, "I'll never say 'I don't need you' to anyone again. We all need each other. I'm living proof of that."

"I LOVE YOU, POP!"

BY
ALBERT DiBARTOLOMEO

After my father died of kidney failure at 35, my mother eventually started dating other men. They showed up loud and jittery, newly barbered and usually smelling too powerfully of cologne. Few of them returned to our house in Philadelphia, and none more than twice. For my two younger sisters and me, they remained only as the butt of jokes or tricks we'd played on them.

One of my mother's dates left his sunglasses in the living room while he had a lemonade in the kitchen. I entertained myself by testing the strength of the frames. They snapped like twigs.

When he returned to the living room, the man pocketed the pieces and abruptly left. My mother said little about what I'd done, understanding better than I the nature of the ill will I harbored in my 14-year-old heart.

Some months later, my sisters came into my room.

"Mom's got a boyfriend," the older one piped.

"What's he like?" I asked.

"He's got a big nose," the eight-year-old said. "That's why his last name is Bananas, because his nose is as big as a banana."

"It's his nickname," my ten-year-old sister added. "He's coming to dinner."

None of the other men had been invited to dinner, and I was old enough to know what this meant. My mother was more serious about Al Bananas than the others.

The following evening, a man with licorice-black hair and the facial lines of Roman statuary stood with complete ease in the middle of our living room. *He does have a big nose,* I thought.

"This is Al," my mother said, nervously wringing a dish towel in her hands. "Al Sbarra."

"My real name's Attilio," the man said amicably, "but everybody calls me Al. Good friends call me Al Bananas." He offered his hand, and I awkwardly shook it, mine feeling small and delicate in his callused plumber's grip.

"We met before," Al said. "I saw you in the hospital when you were a kid. You were in an oxygen tent."

Shortly before my third birthday, I'd come down with severe croup, which so impaired my breathing that I had to undergo an emergency tracheotomy and hovered near death for a week.

"I was a friend of your father's," Al continued. "I gave him a lift to the hospital one day, and I brought you a red firetruck."

"I don't remember you," I told him, unimpressed. But I did remember the truck. It was made of steel and had rubber wheels that spun smoothly. I liked that truck so much that I sometimes slept with it, and I can still recall the coolness of its metal against my cheek and the smell of its enamel.

Al returned to the house several times that spring and summer. A year later, not only was he eating dinner at the house every evening but there was talk of marriage.

I found it difficult to picture Al occupying the same position that my father had, and when I did briefly imagine it, I became irritable.

"I'm never going to call him Dad," I told my sisters.

"Mom says we can call him Pop," the younger one said.

"I'll never call him that either," I answered. To call Al "Pop" would suggest an intimacy that didn't exist between us—nor, I thought, ever would. My father had been distant and often angry, but his presence in the house had been so powerful that I still felt it.

For many years, I regarded Al as merely my mother's friend who showed up at the house around dinner time and who left before ten

o'clock. During that period, Al's estranged first wife refused him a divorce. When he was finally able to marry my mother in 1973, I was living in an apartment, going to college and majoring in English literature. Al was neither more nor less than my mother's second husband.

One early summer night after playing softball, I stopped at our house to say hello. I heard a Frank Sinatra tune as I approached the front door and, looking through a window, saw Al and my mother slow-dancing in the kitchen. I'd never seen my mother and father dance, or show any affection for each other, so I didn't have any memory to compare with this picture of Al and my mother. I waited for the tune to end before entering the house.

Al seemed happy to see me. "There's a laborer's job in Jersey at $2.25 an hour," he said, meaning at the construction site where he worked. "If you want it, come with me tomorrow."

I had been looking for a summer job. "I'm very interested," I told him.

The next morning he picked me up at my apartment at seven o'clock, and we rode in the early sunlight into New Jersey. At the job site

I was assigned to unload dozens of refrigerators and dishwashers from a trailer.

As we drove home after work, Al asked, "So how did it go?"

"Fine," I told him, too tired to elaborate and doubtful that he was actually interested.

He continued to press, then and later, listening as I talked about the work I'd done. Soon he was asking about more than my work. When I began dating the girl who would become my wife, Al surprised me one day by saying, "Your mother says she's very nice. Tell me about her."

I had no idea he knew about her or cared. But his asking about her broke something in me, and our talks became more open.

Al learned what was important to me, and I, well, I already knew what was important to him: work, sports and family.

He'd lived nearly his entire life only a few blocks from the row house in which he was born and raised, and from the houses of his brothers and sisters. That South Philadelphia working-class neighborhood was big and rich enough for him. Our family eventually joined him in South Philly, and on trips through the neighborhood Al proudly introduced me to friends.

"You can never have too many friends," he said during one of our walks. Did he ever desire to live in another place? "Why move away from your family?" he answered.

After that summer ended, Al began to ask me along on side jobs he did once or twice a month on Saturdays. It was a good way for both of us to earn a few extra dollars, and I rarely turned him down, even after graduating from college.

While Al worked, he kept his toolbox within reach and let me perform only the simplest tasks. He seemed to want me to learn his craft by watching and listening. Soon I was making up the materials list and laying out the tools he needed for a job.

At lunch Al sometimes took me to diners where he seemed to know everyone. Once we shared a table with a group of his buddies, to whom he announced that I was "the kid with the genius hands" he had told them about.

One particular Saturday morning, I told Al that, because of budget slashing, I was to be laid off from my regular work as a library assistant.

I wondered aloud, "How am I going to get a job doing what I want to do when I can't even keep a job working at something I don't like?"

Al made no comment until later. "Even if you don't get that job you want, you can always do something to make money," he said. "Don't worry. Everything will work out in the end." He then told me how he'd gotten the name Bananas.

His father, Al said, had peddled bananas in the streets of Philadelphia after he'd lost his job, and he often took Al along with him. Al would run from door to door with a bunch of bananas for sale. Because some of his friends lived behind those doors, they began to call him Al Bananas, a name that stuck.

"My father didn't make much money, but I was sorry when he got another job," he added. "It was nice being with him those times."

I realized then that Al's teaching me a skill and providing me an opportunity to make some money were far less important to him than the time we spent together. Without showing outward affection, Al was fathering me in the only way he knew how, in the way his father had nurtured him. Al had been doing so, really, ever since he'd given me that firetruck when I was a child lying sick in a hospital bed.

Late the following morning, I was feeling feverish. Al came by my apartment to bring me my pay for the work we'd done. "You don't look so good," he said, gazing down at me.

"I don't feel so good."

Where we love

is home.

OLIVER WENDELL HOLMES

"I'll have your mother make you some chicken soup. Anything else I can bring you?"

Without thinking, I said, "How about a red firetruck?"

Al looked baffled—then he smiled. "Sure." When he put my wages on the bedside table, I said, "Thanks . . . Pop."

Some weeks later, Pop telephoned to say he was going to the cemetery to visit his parents' graves and asked if I wanted to come along. He knew that my father was buried in the same place and that I had not been there since the funeral, but he made no mention of this.

After some hesitation, I said, "All right."

Later, inside the cemetery gates, Pop gave me a slight nod and started toward the graves of his parents. I watched him head away and then, tentatively, I set off to find my father.

When I located the grave, I stood a long while and simply gazed at my own last name chiseled in the white stone. Beneath the name were the dates that encapsulated my father's brief life. *The most terrible consequence of his early death,* I thought, *was that I had not known him. Who was he? Did he love me?*

I had not moved when Pop joined me at the grave and put his hand on my shoulder. "Your father was a good man," he said. "He would do anything for you." That compliment freed emotions I'd kept locked away since my father died. As I began to sob, Pop held me.

On the quiet ride home, I began to appreciate what Pop had done. He'd asked me along to the cemetery, it seemed, so I might restore a part of my life that I didn't even know was missing or important until faced with it—my father's memory. He showed me, by joining me at my father's grave, that there was room in my heart for both of them.

In the summer of 1994, Pop woke up with a severe pain in his back. X rays revealed a lung tumor. This and later news that Pop's cancer had spread to his bones devastated us. He'd never been seriously ill in his life.

Pop showed no bitterness. During all the tests, grim reports and radiation treatments, he never complained or lost faith that the doctors would cure him or that God would intervene. The last time I saw him alive, his smile appeared below the tube that fed oxygen to his lungs, and he said, "Don't worry. Everything will work out."

I held his hand as the day and the last of his life faded, and I pictured him beside my hospital bed when I was a child. I wondered if he'd spoken the same words to my father as they looked at me through the plastic of the oxygen tent. Had he somehow glimpsed himself in my future? I don't know, but he did become a vital part of it. Things had indeed worked out by his becoming my Pop.

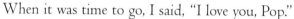

When it was time to go, I said, "I love you, Pop."

He looked up at me through his morphine haze and, nodding slightly, squeezed my hand. There was that smile. He understood.

"So long, Pop," I said. "See you tomorrow." I went out into the chill autumn dusk, holding back tears.

Pop died in his sleep the following afternoon. When I received the news, I was stunned. I couldn't imagine never hearing his voice again and never placing another tool in his strong hands.

Some weeks after the funeral, I went into my mother's basement for a wrench that I needed to replace a washer in her leaky faucet. I opened the toolbox and removed the wrench, but instead of returning with it to the first floor, I held it tightly against my chest. Trembling with fresh grief, I closed my eyes and remembered the many excursions Pop and I had made, not realizing until that moment how much they'd meant to me, while at the same time being enormously grateful that Pop and I had spent that time together.

My mother descended the stairs with a basket of laundry before I moved. She saw me standing in front of the tools with the wrench clutched in my hands.

"Why don't you take the tools home," she said. "Pop would want you to have them. He wouldn't want them sitting here collecting dust."

"No, neither would I." They still retained Pop's essence, and I wanted to be close to that. "Pop was a good man, Mom, and I'm glad you married him."

That was the first time I'd acknowledged Pop's importance in my mother's life. I'd never quite realized until then that she might have needed to hear it much earlier. We embraced there beside the tools before I headed back upstairs to fix the faucet.

I brought Pop's tools home with me that day, and I will treasure them to my own end. But I will cherish more what Pop taught me—to love without selfishness and to forgive the injuries of the past, for only then will our hearts be fully open.

THAT LITTLE
CHINA CHIP

BY

BETTIE B. YOUNGS

One day when I was about nine years old, my mother took a trip into town and put me in charge of my brothers and sisters. As she drove away, I ran into her bedroom and opened the dresser to snoop.

There in the top drawer, beneath soft, wonderful-smelling grown-up garments, was a small wooden jewelry box. I was fascinated by its treasures—the ruby ring left to my mother by her favorite aunt; pearl earrings that once belonged to my grandmother; my mother's own wedding band, which she took off to do farm chores alongside my father.

I tried them all on, filling my mind with glorious images of what it must be like to be a beautiful woman like my mother and to own such exquisite things.

Then I saw there was something tucked behind the piece of red felt lining the lid. Lifting the cloth, I found a little white chip of china.

I picked it up. Why in the world did my mother keep this broken thing? Glinting slightly in the light, it offered no answers.

Some months later, I was setting the dinner table when our neighbor Marge knocked at the door. Mom, busy at the stove, called to her to come in. Glancing at the table, Marge said, "Oh, you're expecting company. I'll stop by another time."

"No, come on in," Mom replied. "We're not expecting anyone."

"But isn't that your good china?" Marge asked. "I'd never trust kids to handle my good dishes!"

Mom laughed. "Tonight's my family's favorite meal. If you set your best table for a special meal with guests, why not for your own family?"

"But your beautiful china!" responded Marge.

"Oh, well," said Mom, "a few broken plates are a small price to pay for the joy we get using them." Then she added, "Besides, every chip and crack has a story to tell."

Reaching into the cupboard, Mom pulled out an old, pieced-together plate. "This one shattered the day we brought Mark home from the hospital," she said. "What a cold and blustery afternoon that was! Judy was only six, but she wanted to be helpful. She dropped the plate carrying it to the sink.

"At first I was upset, but then I told myself, 'I won't let a broken plate change the happiness we feel welcoming our new baby.' Besides, we all had a lot of fun gluing it together!"

Marge looked doubtful.

Mom went to the cupboard again and took down another plate. Holding it up, she said, "See this break on the edge here? It happened when I was 17."

Her voice softened. "One fall day my brothers needed help putting up the last of the hay, so they hired a young man to help out. He was slim, with powerful arms and thick blond hair. He had an incredible smile.

"My brothers took a liking to him and invited him to dinner. When my older brother sat the young man next to me, it flustered me so, I nearly fainted."

Suddenly remembering that she was telling the story to her young daughter and neighbor, Mom blushed and hurried on. "Well, he

handed me his plate and asked for a helping. But I was so nervous that when I took the plate, it slipped and knocked against the casserole dish."

"That sounds like a memory I'd try to forget," said Marge.

"Oh, no," countered my mother. "As the young man was leaving, he walked over, took my hand in his and laid a piece of broken china in my palm. He didn't say a word. He just smiled that smile.

"One year later I married him. And to this day, when I see this plate, I fondly recall the moment I met him."

Seeing me staring, Mom gave me a wink. Then, carefully, she put the plate back, behind the others, in a place all its own.

I couldn't forget about that plate with the missing chip. At the first chance, I went up to Mom's room and took out the little wooden jewelry box again. There was the small shard of china.

I examined it carefully. Then I ran to the kitchen cupboard, pulled over a chair, climbed up and took down the plate. Just as I had guessed, the chip my mother had so carefully saved belonged to the plate she broke on the day she met my father.

Wiser now, and with more respect, I cautiously returned the chip to its place among the jewels.

The love story that began with that chip is now in its fifty-fourth year. Recently one of my sisters asked Mom if someday the antique ruby ring could be hers. My other sister had laid claim to Grandmother's pearl earrings.

As for me, I'd like Mom's most precious keepsake, a memento of an extraordinary life of loving: that little china chip.

There is no more lovely, friendly and
charming relationship, communion or
company than a good marriage.

MARTIN LUTHER

A HANDFUL OF BLACKBERRIES

BY

W. W. MEADE

Just as I began a new job in New York, I had to learn another important job: father. At the office we had three new projects in the works, and at home I had a young son who was growing fast and needed me. To say I felt stretched is an understatement. This was never more clear than one Thursday when, for the second time in a week, I was packing for a business trip.

"I know how important your job is," my wife, Ellen, said. "But it would be nice if you could be home more often."

I knew she was right. My son, Luke, was turning three, and I didn't like being away so much either.

"Yesterday," Ellen said, "Luke wandered around the house saying, 'Where is my dad? Where *is* he?'"

Ellen wanted to discuss this further, but there wasn't time. "Honey, I really have to make this plane," I said. "Let's talk tomorrow when I get back."

In Chicago my meeting ended early, and I suddenly had a couple of hours to kill. So I called on Dan, an old family friend who had retired to the area to be near his grandchildren.

Dan had once farmed in Indiana, where my father was a country doctor. Now, as we sat at his kitchen table, he began to reminisce about what a fine man my dad had been. "He'd get you well no matter what it took," Dan said. "I don't think there was a soul in that county who didn't love your father."

Then, to my surprise, Dan confided that after he'd recovered from prostate cancer, he had developed a serious depression that he just couldn't lick. "I didn't care about getting better," he said. "But your daddy got me through it."

His remembrance touched me, and I put my hand on his shoulder. "He cared about his patients a lot," I agreed.

Indeed, I knew how devoted my father was to his patients. But I also knew that his devotion and hard work came at a price—a price that seemed high to his family.

Dad was a tall, lean man whose sky-blue eyes could see straight through anything. But despite his no-nonsense gaze and way of speaking, he was always easy to talk to.

We lived on a farm, not because we were farmers but because many of my dad's patients were. They often paid in livestock instead of cash, so he found a farm to put his fees out to graze.

There was no denying my father's love of hunting, however, and he always kept bird dogs. I would train them until they were ready to hunt. He left that chore to me, he said, because he didn't have the patience. Yet what he did or did not want to do often seemed to hinge on what I might learn from doing it myself.

My dad taught me everything. He showed me how to use a handsaw and mark a right angle, for instance—skills that enabled me to cobble together a raft for the pond beyond our meadow. One corner ended up out of line, but Dad helped me launch it without comment on its fault.

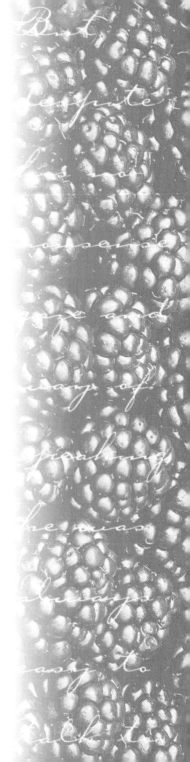

His best way of helping was to ask questions that allowed me to realize things myself. When I was afraid I'd have to fight a guy at school who was hassling me, my father asked, "Can you take him?"

"I think so."

"Then you don't have to. Here, stand up and give me a shove."

He made me push him until I nearly knocked him down. "See, you just have to give him an idea of how strong you are. What if you try that and see if he doesn't back off?" I did, and it worked.

That was the kind of help I needed from Dad. But the summer I turned thirteen, he virtually disappeared from my life, and I didn't know what to do.

So many people were sick, and Dad was gone most of the time seeing patients. He was also building a new office and trying to earn enough to pay for an X-ray machine. Often the phone would ring while we were at supper and I'd hear him say, "Be right there." Then Mom would cover his plate with a pie tin and put it in the oven to wait.

Many more times he'd be gone for an hour or more. Then his car would crunch on the gravel drive, and I'd run downstairs to sit with him while he ate. He'd ask about my day and give me whatever advice I had to have about the farm. But that was about all he had energy for.

As that year went on, I worried about him, and I worried about me. I missed his help. I missed joking around and just being together. *Maybe he doesn't like me as much as he did,* I thought. *Maybe I've done something to disappoint him.* He'd been helping me become a man, and I didn't think I had a prayer of getting that done without his guidance.

The pond beyond the meadow was ringed with reeds and cattails. I liked to fish there. I'd never caught a big one, hooking only sunnies and a few catfish. But big fish were in there. I'd seen them jump, making a glistening turbulence in the mist of early morning. Sometimes the ripples would also carry so far they'd reach the shore.

That summer I used to sit on my raft and think of ways to lure my father back. My mother wanted us to take a vacation, but he nixed that because he had so much work.

One day my mother and I stood in the kitchen and talked about him. "See if you can get him to go fishing," she finally said. "Even just one evening off will help."

The next day I began my campaign to get Dad down to our pond. I planned to make a fire, roast ears of corn and fry up whatever we could catch. The problem was getting my father to change into old clothes and take off a few hours.

Finally one Friday I simply bullied him into it. I met his car when he came home and pulled him into the mudroom, where we changed our work clothes. "We're going fishing," I said. "And that is that."

And we did! As we stood on the pond's edge casting into the fading sunlight, I was still amazed that I'd persuaded him to do it. Soon I went to gather wood for a fire. We hadn't had any luck yet, but we could still roast the corn and talk.

While we worked, I watched him cast into a deep hole near a fallen red oak. "Please let him catch a fish," I whispered to myself. "*Any* fish—just let him catch something."

Almost as if my thought had raised the fish to the lure, a bass struck his line. "Whoa, boss!" he yelled, and the moss-colored fish took to the air. It looked humongous and put up a good fight as Dad expertly reeled it into his net, then brought it to me by the fire.

"Hey, Dad," I said. "How about that!"

He looked young, happy and proud. I dredged his fish in cornmeal and fried it over the fire. We sat on a stone eating our supper.

"That was some meal," he said when finished. "I don't know when I've liked anything more."

My father made a pot of coffee while I went to the edge of the meadow where the briers were borne down with ripe blackberries. I picked up our

A happy family is but an earlier heaven.

JOHN BOWRING

55

dessert and carried it back in my baseball cap. We had the berries with our coffee and watched the sun make dazzling colors in the western sky. My father ate slowly, one berry at a time, savoring each. Then out of the blue he began telling me how much he cared about me.

"You know, Son, you're going to be a success in life," he said. "I know that because I never have to ask you to do something twice. But more than that, you're a good kid."

The expression on his face was of such warmth and pride that I felt utterly blessed.

Times like this were all too rare as my father's practice grew ever larger. But whenever I needed to, I'd reach back to that moment by the pond, remembering how good it felt when Dad was with me.

"Yes, sir," Dan said, interrupting my memories. "Your father was some fine man. And his medicine wasn't just pills and shots. He thought a lot about people. He could always understand what someone was going through."

"Yes. Sometimes he did," I said, looking momentarily away.

Then Dan told me: "When I was at my worst, I said to him, 'Doc, give me one good reason to beat this depression.' And do you know what he said?"

Dan stared across the table until I re-established eye contact. "He said, 'Blackberries. Think of a handful of blackberries and how wonderful that is. To pick a handful of blackberries, sit down with someone you love very much and eat them. Think of that and tell me life's not worth the fight. You have a wonderful wife and three fine kids. Take some time with them. It's family we live for—not just ourselves.'

"That's what he said, and I've never forgotten it," Dan finished. "I think it saved my life."

My hands were quivering. All I could do was stare back at him. I was feeling so many emotions that I could not muster one word.

On the plane home I closed my eyes and thought about me and my dad. I knew what that day by the pond meant to me. But I had never known what it meant to him. Now, in my mind's eye, I could see him standing at the edge of the water, the bass on his line, so full of joy. *How wide the ripples spread*, I thought. *How far they reach.*

Suddenly I found myself staring out the airplane window, hoping that the flight would get in on time. I planned to be home before dark for a change—to play in the yard with my son in the fading light of day.

A HOUSEFUL OF LOVE
AND LAUGHTER

BY

JAY LENO

Biologically speaking, I came late to the party. When I was born, my mother was 41, my dad was 42 and my brother was already ten. This built-in generation gap probably defined me every bit as much as my distinctly peculiar blood mix.

My mother, Catherine, was born in Scotland. My father, Angelo, was a first-generation Italian-American. I seem to be divided right down the middle. My Scottish side is practical, analytical, even a bit frugal. My Italian side is loud, outgoing, ready to laugh (and be laughed at).

As an immigrant, my mother lived in constant fear of deportation. You could miss up to four questions on the citizenship test, and Mom missed five. The question she flunked on was: "What is the Constitution of the United States?" The answer she gave was: "A boat."

Which wasn't entirely wrong. The USS *Constitution* was docked in Boston. But the judge instantly denied her citizenship.

My father stormed up to the judge. "What the hell is this? Let me see the test! She's not wrong—the *Constitution* is a boat!"

The judge rolled his eyes and said, "No, the Constitution is our basic governing—"

"It's also a boat in Boston! The *Constitution!* Same thing! Come on!"

The judge finally couldn't take any more. He said, "Fine. She's a *citizen.* Now get out of here!"

So my father said to my mom, "You passed!"

"No, I didn't pass," she whimpered. "They're going to come after me!" From then on, any time my mother was even in the proximity of a policeman, she quaked with fear. When I took her to Scotland in 1983, she asked me, "Will I be able to get back in?"

"Ma! Don't worry! That was 50 years ago! They don't know that you said *a boat!*" It never ended.

My First Fish Story. My father always tried to get me to do outdoorsy things. He'd say, "Why don't you go fishing?" Fishing, to me, was like a nap with a stick.

"Just go," my mother told me. "If you catch one fish, you can at least show your father that you tried."

One day at school I heard they were draining a lake near our house and there were all these fish flopping around. So I rode my bike over and scooped up about 25.

I walked in the house and said, "Hey, Pop! Look what I caught!"

My father just beamed with pride. "Hey! Look at my boy! Look at all the fish he got there!"

Mom cut them open and started gagging. "These fish stink!" she said. "We can't eat them!"

"Oh, I'm sure they're fine!" Dad said. "What a little fisherman!"

My mother finally took me aside, and I confessed under threat of frying pan: "Okay, okay—I found 'em! They were all dead!" Mom was exasperated, but so as not to disappoint my dad, she ran out to the store and bought fresh fish, which she served that night. Dad never found out.

The Tape Is Rolling. When I was in high school, my brother Pat was drafted into the Army and sent to Vietnam. Nobody in the family was much of a letter writer, so my father had the idea to get a miniature tape recorder to make voice messages.

The clerk at the electronics store asked, "How long a tape do you want—15 minutes?"

"*Fifteen minutes!*" Dad said. "We couldn't even say hello in 15 minutes! What's your *longest* tape?"

"Ninety minutes."

"That's more like it! Give me four!"

At home my father set up everything on the kitchen table and announced, "Okay, now we're all gonna talk to Pat!" He pressed the record button and in his own inimitable way began: "HELLO, PAT! EVERY-THING HERE IS GOOD! I'M FINE! YOUR MOTHER'S FINE! HERE'S YOUR BROTHER! JAMIE, TALK TO PAT!"

I stepped forward: "Hey, Pat! How you doing? Hope you're okay! Be careful over there! Here's Mom!"

Mom bent over the machine and said, "Hello, Pat! Take care of yourself now! Don't do anything silly!"

Then my dad: "HEY, WHERE'S THE DOG? BRING BRUCE OVER HERE AND MAKE HIM BARK!"

Bruce barked: "Roof roof roof!"

Then, of course, my father had to point out, "THAT'S THE DOG THERE, PAT! THAT'S BRUCE THE DOG!"

We put all of about three minutes on this 90-minute tape. The next day, the same thing: "PAT, EVERYTHING IS GOOD! HERE'S THE DOG!"

"Roof roof! Roof roof!"

After a few weeks there was no more than nine minutes of tape filled, mostly the dog. Finally my father said, "Oh, let's just send the tape! What the hell!" So we shipped the whole contraption off to my brother. Thinking back, I have a feeling he might have preferred a few letters.

"Quiet, Please!" Until *The Tonight Show* became a full-time job, I spent most of every year playing one-nighters in every state of the nation. My life mystified my mother. For the longest time, she never quite understood what I did.

In 1986 I played Carnegie Hall, which my parents wouldn't have missed for the world. The ushers took them to their seats, fifth row center. When I started doing my material, the crowd couldn't have been more receptive. My mother didn't know what to make of such laughter. At one point she turned around, pressed a finger to her lips and went, *"Shhhh! Quiet!"*

I saw this from the stage. "Ma! Don't shush! It's a comedy show! They're *supposed* to laugh!"

This mortified her. To be singled out in public was the worst embarrassment imaginable. And at Carnegie Hall yet!

I always told my dad if I ever made it in show business, I'd buy him a Cadillac. So as soon as I started guest-hosting for Johnny Carson, I took Dad shopping. The salesman led him directly to a new white Caddy with a red velour interior. Dad wanted it on sight.

We drove it home to show my mom, who deplored ostentatiousness of any kind. She came out to meet us in the driveway and covered her eyes with shame when she saw the red velour. To her it looked like a brothel on wheels.

From that day on, when they rode around in the Cadillac, she would slump down so people wouldn't see her while my father honked at everyone in town and hollered, "HEY, MY BOY BOUGHT THIS FOR ME!"

A Lifetime Warranty. My father loved warranties. For every product he ever bought, he would fill out the warranty card and make a copy—"for our files." Just in case.

Once when I was home for a visit, the toilet seat broke off. The hinge was rusty, and I went to throw out the seat.

My dad said, "Wait! Don't throw that away! I've got a 20-year guarantee on that thing!"

Within minutes he pulled out the warranty—a yellowed piece of paper that looked like the Magna Carta.

I said, "Put that away, Dad! I am not walking down Main Street with this rotted-out toilet seat!"

"Then *I'll* do it. I've got a guarantee!"

So I drove him over to the hardware store with this awful old seat. The guy who sold it to us had retired ten years earlier. His son came out.

Dad said, "My toilet seat broke. I want a new one."

The guy looked and said, "It's rotted! I can't give you a new one."

So my dad presented him with the warranty. "Oh, yeah? Look at this! Ninety-two days left!"

The guy gave us a new seat.

The warranty on the new toilet seat promised it would last until the year 2008. When we got home, he filled out the card and made a big show of putting it in my name. This was my inheritance.

One last story ought to give you a good idea of exactly what kind of parents they were.

When I was a teenager, I scraped up money to buy an old Ford pickup. Every day after school I worked on it—sanding, painting, buffing. As a present, my parents got me brand-new Naugahyde upholstery for the seats.

Then once I slammed a door a little too hard, and the window shattered. I didn't have any money to replace it. I drove it anyway, including to school.

My high school was a big flat building, and you could see the parking lot from many of the classrooms. One day it began to rain. I sat in class and watched my truck—and new upholstery—get drenched through the broken window.

Suddenly I saw my mom and dad tear into the parking lot. They screeched up next to my truck and dragged a huge piece of plastic out of their car. Then, in the pouring rain, they covered up the truck.

Dad had left his office in the middle of the day, picked up Mom and bought this hunk of plastic to save my seats. I watched them do this. And I just began crying right there in class.

My parents were with me through every high and low in my life, always supportive and proud of my accomplishments. I never think of them as gone. I've got all their stories, and that keeps them nearby always.

GIRL AGAINST A BLIZZARD

BY

HELEN REZATTO

The morning of March 15 was pleasant and sunny as William Miner, a farmer near Center, North Dakota, completed his chores. A thaw had set in, and the snow in the fields was patchy.

"Snow should be gone by night," he reported optimistically to his wife when he came in at noon. After the couple had eaten a leisurely meal, Miner glanced out the kitchen window. "Good Lord!" he exclaimed.

In the northwest a black, billowy cloud loomed over the horizon. It moved stealthily, inexorably, its dark bluish edges spreading across the sky toward the unsuspecting sun.

Blanche Miner spoke with the sure instinct of a homesteader. "A spring norther!"

They watched the advance of the formless, faceless monster. Abruptly, Miner said, "You get the stock in. I'm going to school to get the kids. I don't like the looks of it."

Miner piled on his storm clothes, saddled Kit, his best horse, and started down the slushy road to the school two and a half miles away.

By now the apparition had writhed and swelled its way to overpower the sun. All nature was poised, breathless, apprehensive. Then an avalanche of blinding snow and wind slammed into the horse and rider. Miner fought through it to the school barn, tied Kit among the other stomping, nervous horses, and hurried into the schoolhouse.

The teacher and pupils had observed the approach of the blizzard, but were still pretending to concentrate on their lessons. Although many children had their own horses and sleighs in the school barn, the established blizzard rule was that no child should leave unless called for by a parent.

"Hi, Dad!" 15-year-old Hazel Miner exclaimed. She turned to her brother, Emmet, 11, and her sister Myrdith, 8. "I guess *somebody* doesn't trust us to drive old Maude home!"

Her father smiled briefly. "Hurry! Get your wraps—here are extra scarves."

Hazel bent down to fasten her sister's overshoes and said to Emmet, "Don't forget your history book." Hazel was wonderfully dependable, Miner thought. She always far surpassed expectations.

He carried Myrdith outside to their homemade sleigh with its rounded canvas cover, settled the two children in the straw lining the bottom, covered them with two blankets and an old fur robe. Then Hazel perched on the driver's seat while her father hitched Maude to the sleigh. Above the belligerent wind he shouted to Hazel, "Stay right here! I'll get Kit and lead the way."

Maude was facing the north gate toward home. She had always been placid and easily managed, but now a thunderclap startled her, and she bolted, swerving through the south gate. Hazel, knocked off balance and hardly able to see through the swirling snow, did not realize at first that Maude was headed in the wrong direction. She shouted to the wide-eyed younger children, "Don't worry, we'll beat Dad and Kit home! Maude knows the way."

Hazel could do nothing to control the horse, for the reins trailed out of reach beneath the tugs. Finally, Maude slowed to a walk and stopped, her sides heaving.

Emmet called, "Are we home? Did we beat Dad?"

Hazel stepped down into the snow. Through the dizzying gloom she could not tell whether they were on a road or in a field. The whole world had become a white-foaming, lashing sea, threatening to swallow them all. Panting for breath, she crawled back into the driver's seat with the reins. "No, we're not home yet, but I think we're close. Now that Maude's calmed down, she'll know the way."

Maude, repentant about her escapade, plowed through the growing gloom. Once she plunged into a low place filled with water from the spring thaws and choked with ice and new snow. A tug came unhitched, and Hazel stepped down into the chilling slush, reached her bare hands into the water, fumbled for the tug, fastened it. By the time she led Maude out of the water, she was soaked to the waist and her clothes were turning into heavy armor.

Then, close by, she saw the top of a fence post sticking above the snow. She dug into the snow until she located the barbed wire. The fence would lead them to a farm and safety.

Emmet got out to see what she was doing. Together, they broke off the crystal mask that had formed over Maude's face. They grasped Maude's bridle to keep her on the fence line, but a huge drift blocked the way and they had to turn off the course. Frantically trying to get back, Emmet and Hazel pawed for the wire or another post to guide them. They could find neither. (The gate, buried in the big drift, opened to a farm only 200 feet away.)

Almost suffocated from the onslaught of wind and snow, the two climbed back into the sleigh. Stubbornly, Maude kept on until the sleigh lurched over a concealed obstacle. It tipped over on its side, and the children were thrown against the canvas top.

Again Hazel and Emmet got out. Blindly, they pushed, they heaved, they pulled. The sleigh, jammed into the snow, was too heavy for them to right.

In the howling darkness, Hazel realized that she must think—it was up to her, the oldest. She fumbled inside the canvas. "See," she said, "we're in a little cave. We'll fix it nice and cozy."

Since the sleigh was on its side, the narrow wooden floor formed a low wall to the east, and the canvas top, uncurtained at the ends, made a tunnel-like tent. In the dark, Hazel found the blankets and robe. Despite her now-crippled hands, she placed the two blankets on the canvas "floor." Following her instructions, Emmet and Myrdith lay down, curled together tightly. The wind snarled through the north opening, and Hazel tried to improvise a curtain with the fur robe. It blew down again and again. Finally she tucked the robe around her brother and sister.

The hellish wind tore and ripped at the canvas top. Hazel snatched at the flapping scraps and piled over the robe all she could salvage. There was only one way to keep them in place—to fling herself on top of them. Now there was nothing between the three children and the blizzard except some dangling strips blowing from the bare wooden framework.

The snow fell incessantly. Three human specks lay motionless, their minds and bodies stupefied, benumbed by the terrifying, pulsating forces. Hazel roused herself. "Emmet! Myrdith!" she shouted. "You mustn't close your eyes. Punch each other! I'll count to a hundred. Make your legs go up and down as though you're running. Begin—one, two, three—" She could feel the small limbs moving underneath her. She tried to move her own; her brain instructed her legs, but she wasn't sure what they did.

"I'm tired. Can't we stop?" begged Myrdith's muffled voice.

"No!" came the stern answer. "We're only at 71."

Next Hazel ordered, "Open and close your fingers 100 times inside your mittens."

Emmet stuck his head out from under the robe. "Come on, Hazel, get under here. We'll make room."

"No, I can't." Little warmth her ice-mantled clothes would provide the others. "Everything blows away. I've got to hold it down. Besides, I'm not very cold. Let's sing 'America the Beautiful' like in opening exercises the morning."

From underneath the robe came the thin, childish voices and the words they had sung only that morning—but a hundred years away. *For purple mountains majesties above the fruited plain.* They sang all four verses.

"Let's pray to God to help us," suggested Myrdith. " 'Now I lay me down to sleep—' " she began.

Hazel interrupted, "No, not that one. Let's say 'Our Father' instead." Solemnly they chanted the prayer.

On into the timeless night Hazel directed them—in exercises, stories, songs, prayers. Several times she sat up in the never-ending snow and forced her nearly paralyzed fingers to break the crusts that formed around Myrdith's and Emmet's legs; then she brushed and scraped away the creeping menace.

She said to the two children over and over, "Remember, you mustn't go to sleep—even if I do. Promise me you won't, no matter how sleepy you get. *Keep each other awake!* Promise?"

They promised.

More than once Myrdith voiced the question: "Why doesn't Daddy find us?"

When William Miner discovered his children had disappeared from the schoolyard, he urged Kit mercilessly through the fast-forming drifts, sure that Maude had gone home. His wife met him at the door. They gazed, stricken, into each other's eyes.

Immediately, he gave the alarm over the rural party lines. Nearly 40 men, risking their lives, were soon moving slowly, persistently, over the fields and roads between Miner's farm and the school. They paused at farms to change teams, to treat frostbite, to gulp coffee, to devise new plans. All the other children were safe in their homes. The men found nothing.

The wind became a 60-mile-an-hour gale, the temperature dropped to zero, the gray became utter blackness. And the maddening snow kept falling. The searchers had to give up until daylight.

Next morning one group of searchers reported tracks made by a small sleigh and a horse which went out the south schoolhouse gate—then were obliterated by the falling snow. Quickly, the search was reorganized. Men with teams and sleighs, men on horseback, men on foot fanned out for half a mile. Back and forth they forced their way across the shrouded land.

At two o'clock on Tuesday afternoon, 25 hours from the time the Miner children had disappeared, searchers spotted something in a pasture two miles south of the school. It was an overturned sleigh. Next to it, like a sentry, a ghostlike horse stood motionless but still alive. They saw a bulky snow-covered mound under the arch of the naked, skeleton-like staves.

The rigid body of a girl lay face down with her unbuttoned coat flung wide. Her arms were outstretched over her brother and sister, sheltering and embracing them in death as she had in life.

Tenderly, the men lifted her, then slowly removed the matted robe and torn canvas pieces that she had been holding down with her body. Underneath were Myrdith and Emmet, dazed and partially frozen but alive. They had promised never to fall into the dread sleep from which Hazel knew they could never waken.

Today, on the courthouse grounds in the town of Center, these words are engraved on a granite monument rising, like a challenge, above the plains:

In

Memory

of

Hazel Miner

April 11, 1904

March 16, 1920

To the dead a tribute

To the living a memory

To posterity an inspiration

The story of her life and of her

Tragic death is recorded in the

archives of Oliver County.

Stranger, read it

For there is no friend like a sister

In calm or stormy weather;

To cheer one on the tedious way,

To fetch one if one goes astray,

To lift one if one totters down,

To strengthen whilst one stands.

CHRISTINA ROSSETTI

SURROUNDED BY BROTHERS

BY

JAMES SCHEMBARI

I know it is wrong to envy your children. But when I see my son Tonio and his younger brother Sam going down a slide together, one's arms around the other, I know I have missed something wonderful.

Not only did I never have a brother, but I also had no friendships like theirs. There was no Huck to my Tom. My sister was old enough to help take care of me, so she was more a mother than a playmate, and I was more a pest than a friend. A brother would have been terrific, but it was not in the family planning.

My parents worked side by side in their own little business. My mom said she was willing to have another child if, for this one, she could stay home from work. My father said he couldn't manage without her. I don't think they ever discussed it again.

Now I finally live with brothers, my sons, and I am watching them forge the kind of relationship that I once daydreamed about. I have a picture of Tonio with his head on my pregnant wife's belly the night Sam was born. Tonio, only 18 months old, had been talking to the baby, and he had his ear pressed against my wife, listening for an answer. The boys have been whispering to each other ever since.

Sam, oddly, manages the world with more ease than his older brother, whose frustrations often bring him to tears. With an earnest "Smile, Tonio," Sam is the one who comforts him. They are always backing each other up.

Tonio has stopped playing with boys his age who don't want Sam tagging along, explaining, "They called Sam a baby." I cannot punish one without angering the other. "Leave Sam alone," Tonio insolently tells me when I yell at his brother. "You made Tonio cry," Sam scolds me when I get after Tonio.

They go to bed, one in the top bunk, the other in the bottom. By morning they are in one bed, curled up around each other like puppies in a box. When one comes into our bed after a nightmare, my wife and I know that before morning his brother will follow.

When Sam used to take long afternoon naps, Tonio would mope around the house until Sam awoke. Once, I caught him standing by the bed, poking his finger into Sam, whispering, "Sammy, Sammy," trying to wake him up.

In nursery school, Tonio would hold Sam's hand and walk him to class before running into his own. When Tonio's classmates filed out to go to the playground, Sam would run to the door of his classroom and shout, "Hi, Tonio." Tonio would grin, and the boys would wave.

I don't know what kind of relationship they will have when they grow up. Parents always want their children to have what they never could. I want them always to have each other. So I imagine them going to the same college, marrying sisters, and living on the same block.

Sitting just out of the way, I often watch them, imagining what my own brother would have been like. I feel foolish, getting deeper into middle age, conjuring up an imaginary playmate, but my sons show me what could have been. That must be why I had dreaded the day Tonio started kindergarten. I felt that I would lose something too.

As we headed for school that morning, both boys seemed relaxed, as if neither had any idea that the day was going to be different, that starting then, Tonio would be leaving behind his brother, his best friend, his right arm.

Tonio's first day was chaotic, with hundreds of children outside look-

ing for their teachers. My daughter, Marian, a third-grader, took off to find her friends, and before any of us could say good-bye, Tonio disappeared with his new classmates. He turned to wave and then was gone.

It was so sudden. Sam didn't even see him go. Although parents had been asked to ease the craziness of the first day by staying out of the school, I lifted Sam up and took him to Tonio's classroom. We stood just outside of the door, looking for a glimpse of Tonio. Sam spotted him first.

"Tonio!" Sam shouted, but his bewildered brother didn't even look up. There was too much noise.

"Can I go in?" Sam asked. I hesitated. The teacher would kill me. "No," I finally said. "We're not allowed to today. Maybe we can come back tomorrow." Sam quietly rested his head against my shoulder as we left the school.

My wife and I didn't head back home immediately, stopping instead at a coffee shop to treat Sam to hot chocolate. We even let him eat the whipped cream with his fingers. Sam was still quiet, so I asked him if he missed his brother already.

He didn't answer. Instead he asked, "Daddy, is Tonio going to be gone forever?"

"No, Sammy," I said, brightening at the sweetness of his question. "Not forever, just until three o'clock."

Sam licked more whipped cream from his fingers, looking puzzled. Then he asked, "Is that forever?"

On that day, at least, forever lasted only till one P.M., when Tonio was sent home with a fever. Sam wanted to play, but Tonio was too sick. The next morning, after a listless breakfast, he said he was tired and went upstairs to his room. He didn't go to school.

When I poked my head into their room to check on Tonio, he was asleep. And there playing with a toy to pass the time was Sam, snuggled under the covers next to him. Sam was waiting for his brother to wake up, probably relieved at how tolerable forever turned out to be.

I sometimes think that the greatest thing I have ever done is to help create these brothers. And I didn't stop with them. We had another child, and for the third time in a row, it was a boy. It wasn't long before the bottom of his crib cracked from the weight of his older brothers, who climbed in to play with him. I am surrounded by brothers.

It is better than I ever imagined.

SEARCH FOR A STRANGER

BY

GORDON S. LIVINGSTON, M.D.

The highly emotional events of last summer were triggered by the most prosaic of questions: a cousin I was visiting asked me how my work was going. I am a child psychiatrist in Columbia, Maryland, and I answered his question by telling about a recent conference I had attended which had considered the process of adoption, its joys and problems. I told him how I had headed a workshop on behavior difficulties in adopted children, which concluded that such children may experience a disproportionate number of emotional problems requiring professional help.

"One of the factors," I said, "may be the child's burden of 'dual identity,' which is made worse by the secrecy surrounding the adoption process. In all states but four, courts and social agencies are permitted to seal the records. When an adopted child tries to find out the truth about himself and comes upon all this secrecy, he often concludes there is something shameful about him."

"But why do they need to know they're adopted?" my cousin asked.

"It's a very difficult secret to keep, and if a child learns of it from sources other than his parents, there can be psychological damage. Better that he knows the truth from the beginning." I cited a number of case histories. And, as the father of four, I spoke of efforts to be truthful to Michael, our youngest, who is adopted.

"But what if Michael someday wants to meet his real parents?" my cousin argued. "You won't feel any jealousy?"

"No. His desire to know his biological heritage will not alter our basic loving relationship."

My cousin shook his head in disbelief. "What would you do if you yourself were adopted?"

"I'd search for my natural parents," I said promptly.

"Well, start looking," he said.

At first I thought he was joking. When it became evident that he was not, it was as though some unseen fist had struck a blow to the pit of my stomach. I tried to compose myself, forcing deep, even breathing.

"You all right?" my cousin asked.

"I'm fine," I assured him. I was far from fine. I felt I had lost an important part of my identity. All the basic facts about myself that I had taken for granted were suddenly stripped away. If I was not Scotch-Irish, as I had supposed, what nationality was I? Raised as an only child, did I actually have brothers and sisters? Who were my natural parents? The alienation the adopted can feel when not prepared for the truth, and the need for a biologic identity, were no longer theories, abstractions: they were real problems—they were mine!

When I confronted my adoptive father late that night—Mother had died the year before—he looked crushed. "We never told you," he said, "because we were afraid you'd want to meet your real parents and we might lose you."

I put my hand on his arm. "You and Mom *are* my real parents. You loved me and raised me . . . and I love you. Nothing can change that."

He gave me a grateful though tremulous smile and said, "Well, if you feel you must search for them I'll help you all I can."

My birth certificate listed me as being born in Memphis, Tennessee, on June 30, 1938. Dad thought the birth date was correct but could not remember the name of the Memphis agency that had arranged the adoption. He and Mother lived in Detroit at the time and had gone to Memphis with friends named Martin who had also adopted a child. It was a thin lead, but after a dozen phone calls I traced the Martins to California and learned from them that the agency was the Tennessee Children's Home Society.

There was no phone listing for such an agency, so I wrote to the Tennessee Department of Public Welfare and asked permission to see the records of the Tennessee Children's Home Society. The reply was brief: "The Tennessee adoption law prohibits the reopening of closed adoption records except upon an order from the court in which the adoption was granted."

I arranged with colleagues to care for my patients during my absence, then drove to the Laurel, Maryland, airport where I hangared my single-engine Cessna airplane. After takeoff I set a course toward Memphis 800 miles west-southwest. As I watched the highways and farms and rivers and cities stretch to the horizon, I realized how remote the chance was of finding my mother. In that vast land I sought a single person whose face I would not recognize, whose name I did not know.

There was no record of the Tennessee Children's Home Society in the Memphis city hall. I went to a local newspaper and asked to see their back issues. I almost wished I hadn't—for I discovered that in the fall of 1950, the Home had been put out of business by court order! The front-page story revealed that the director had been selling children for high fees and pocketing the money. She had marketed the babies of unwed mothers, prostitutes, mental patients. I stared hard at the paper. In which of these categories was I?

The next day I engaged a local lawyer to help in the search. Twenty-four hours later he telephoned. "I found you in the Bureau of Vital Statistics," he said. "Your birth name was Donald Alfred Cardell. The sealed records are in the Memphis courthouse. We can try to get a look at them tomorrow." For the rest of that day and a good deal of the night I repeated the name over and over.

The next morning we had a stroke of luck—my lawyer knew the courthouse clerk and when he casually asked for the record of the adoption proceedings, an envelope was delivered to us. With trembling hands I removed a legal document and spread it before us. It was an adoption decree, headed "Probate Court of Shelby County, 17th day of August, 1940." My mother's name was Ann Simmons Cardell. Nothing about my father. The document stated that "the child is destitute and helpless," that "the father has abandoned the child." This could only mean that I was illegitimate. I felt a rush of sympathy for that unwanted child of so many years ago.

"I'd like a copy of my adoption decree," I said to the lawyer. The clerk, suddenly realizing my identity, grabbed the paper out of my hands. "Only the judge can give you permission to see this," she said sharply. But I had seen enough.

Armed with the name, my lawyer made the rounds of the hospitals and finally found a listing of my mother's admission. She was a schoolteacher from Mississippi.

Again I was in the air, heading south toward Jackson, the capital of Mississippi.

There is not so much comfort in the having of children as there is sorrow in parting with them.

THOMAS FULLER, M.D.

When I landed, I hired a car and asked directions to the Department of Education. But though I was given complete access to the files, at the end of a long day's work I had found no Ann Cardell in the listings of teachers. Discouraged, I started to leave the dusty stacks when I noticed an old filing case marked "Academic Records." I opened it and found yellowed manila folders, one of which carried the neatly lettered words, ANN SIMMONS CARDELL. It revealed that my mother had received a master's degree in education in 1952, and gave the name of the college where she had earned it.

From a phone booth I called the college's alumni office and asked if Ann Cardell's address was on their current alumni-letter mailing list. "I'm sorry, sir, but the last correspondence this office had from Miss Cardell was over ten years ago. From Natchez. She may be deceased."

Back at the airport I filed my flight plan for Natchez.

The phone book at the Natchez airport showed six Cardells, none of them Ann. The first one listed was Alfred Cardell, Jr. When he answered the phone, I said, "My mother knew an Ann Cardell back in college. I promised her that if I ever came to Natchez I'd look her up. Did you ever know an Ann Cardell?"

"She's my aunt," he replied. "She lives in Savannah."

"I'd appreciate her address," I said, as calmly as I could. "I just may be in Savannah sometime soon."

It was seven in the evening when I landed in Savannah, parked the Cessna and stepped into a phone booth. The phone rang twice. "Hello?"

"Ann Cardell?" I asked.

"Yes."

"Miss Cardell, my name is Gordon Livingston. I've thought a good deal about how to out this, but I haven't come up with any way but simply to say it. I'm your son. I've come a long way. I would very much like to meet you."

There was a pause before she answered, in a southern accent which unaccountably surprised me. "Yes," she said. "There are many things I would like to talk to you about."

When I arrived at the address I found an apartment on a well-groomed street. In response to my knock, the door opened and there stood an attractive and dignified woman in her sixties. From behind glasses she looked at me cautiously. She was a stranger. "Please come in," she said.

Coffee had been made and when I accepted a cup I heard the china make a tinkling sound in her trembling hands. After some awkward amenities, I said that I would like to know about her and my father. She began to speak in a low, guarded voice. She had been born in 1912 to a farm family in Mississippi. By frugal living her parents were able to send her to college. She taught first and third grades in Mississippi for some 20 years, then retired to take a job as an administrator in the school system of a neighboring state.

When she began to speak of my birth her voice was full of emotion. "Back in those days, in a small southern community, the disgrace of being pregnant and unmarried . . . it was more than I could face . . . more than I could ask my family to face." She continued in a monotone. "It was during my first year of teaching. Your father was older, 28, a most handsome man, a marvelous dancer. He was the only man I ever loved . . . before or since. When I learned I was pregnant I begged him to marry me and give my baby a clear name. He said we'd have to think about things. I never saw him again. I went to Memphis to have my baby and no one back home ever knew anything about it. Three years ago I read that he . . . your father . . . died of cancer."

That was the end of the story, the end of my search. It was not an unusual story in many ways—a one-sided love affair, a young woman bereft and with child. But this was our story, hers and mine, and across the years I could feel the shame and confusion of that young schoolteacher as she faced the decision which would separate her from me.

Her feelings of remorse were deep. "It's been the bitter regret of my life that I lost my baby because of my own cowardice," she said. "But I had my own way of keeping track of your development as a child. I knew that in 1944 you would be six years old and in the first grade. I could hardly wait for my own class of '44. When I gave I.Q. tests I hoped the brightest one was you; when I comforted a defeated child I feared that he might be you."

A remembering smile touched her face. "You did everything at top speed that year. You were aggressive, yet vulnerable and easily wounded by a harsh word. I learned that you needed an atmosphere of tolerance and love. I tried to give it to you by giving it to all those children.

"It was an illusion, of course, but I half believed it, and when it came time for me to say good-bye to that class in the spring, I felt sick with guilt. It was as if I were abandoning you the second time.

"Then, during the following winter, there came the news that the third-grade teacher was retiring. I immediately petitioned the school board for a transfer to that grade and it was granted. I would again be your teacher, this time when you were eight.

"That year, as I watched you mature, I was proud that you were becoming your own man but also hurt that the ties between us were loosening. By the end of that year, I was determined to put you out of my mind, for I knew I was being very selfish. Still, I always wanted my

Children are the anchors that hold a mother to life.

SOPHOCLES

82

child back. As I grew older, I prayed that I would one day meet him as a man . . . so I could ask his forgiveness."

My throat tightened and tears stung my eyes. Forgive her? The very idea that I should judge her was outrageous. I stood woodenly, immobilized by my emotions. She made the first move. Slowly, humbly, she held out her arms. For the first time in 37 years I touched my mother and she touched me.

WHY I WEAR A PLASTIC DINOSAUR

BY

DAN SCHAEFFER

was pulling out of my driveway to do an errand when I saw my son running toward me, his eyes aglow with excitement. "I've got a present for you, Daddy."

"Really?" I said, frustrated at the delay. He opened his fingers to reveal a five-year-old's treasures. "I found them for you." What lay in those small hands was a marble, an old metal race car, a broken rubber band and several other things I can't recall. "Take them, Daddy—they're for you," he gushed with pride.

"I can't right now, son. I've got to go somewhere. Why don't you put them in the garage for me?"

His smile fell, and from the moment I drove off I felt remorse. Later, on returning, I asked my son, "Where are those neat toys you had for me?"

"I didn't think you wanted them so I gave them to Adam." Adam lives down the street, and I could picture that little boy accepting those treasures with more gratitude than I had. My son's decision hurt, but I deserved it—not simply because it highlighted my thoughtless reaction to his gesture, but because it triggered memories of another little boy.

It was his sister's birthday, and the youngster had been given two dollars to buy something for her at the five-and-dime. He toured the toy department repeatedly—the gift had to be special. Finally he saw it: a plastic bubble-gum machine filled with brightly colored treasures. He wanted to show it to her as soon as he got it home but valiantly resisted.

Later, at the birthday party attended by her friends, the boy's sister began to open her gifts. With each one she squealed with delight—and with each squeal the boy felt more apprehensive. These eight-year-olds could afford to spend more than two dollars. His package now seemed smaller and less significant. Yet he remained eager to see her eyes sparkle as she opened it. After all, she hadn't received anything she could eat or collect pennies in.

When she finally opened his present, he saw her disappointment—even embarrassment. To maintain her standing among her peers, she couldn't acknowledge the gift with too much enthusiasm.

She smiled knowingly at her friends. "Thanks," she said to her brother in a patronizing tone. "It's just what I wanted." Several girls tried unsuccessfully to contain giggles.

The boy was hurt and confused. What had seemed so beautiful now looked like the plastic, cheap thing that it was. He walked outside to the back porch and began to cry.

Soon his mother appeared and asked gently what was wrong. He explained as best he could.

She listened, then went inside. In a few moments, his sister appeared. He could tell by her expression that she'd been sent, but her genuine remorse reminded him that she hadn't intended to be mean. She really did like his bubble-gum toy. He said he understood, and he did. She was just being nice.

Now things had come full circle. Instead of my sister and me, it was my son who would decide for himself if it really is the thought that counts. And my response would play a large part in his decision.

That Christmas my children were given money to buy presents at a school crafts fair. They tried hard to keep from telling me what I was to receive—especially my son. Not a day went by that he didn't make me guess what it might be.

On Christmas morning he insisted I open his package first. I unwrapped it and looked inside—it was truly the most beautiful present I'd ever received. But I was no longer looking at it through jaded 33-year-old eyes. Instead, I looked at it through excited five-year-old eyes.

My gift was a small, green plastic dinosaur of the *Tyrannosaurus rex* variety. My son quickly pointed out its best feature: its front claws were also clips, so you could wear it all the time. His eyes were filled with expectation and love—the kind found only in very young eyes.

I knew how he must have agonized at the fair to find a gift that would best communicate his feelings for me. So I responded the way a five-year-old would understand. I clipped it on my lapel and raved how "cool" it was and, yes, he was right—I did love it.

So the next time you see an adult wearing a crude paper tie or a "cool" five-cent (removable) caterpillar tattoo, don't bother feeling sorry for him. If you tell him he looks silly, he'll say, "Maybe, but I've got a five-year-old son who thinks I'm the best thing since peanut butter, and there isn't enough money in the U.S. Treasury to make me take it off."

And that's why I wear a plastic dinosaur.

We find delight in the beauty and happiness

of children that makes the heart too big for

the body.

RALPH WALDO EMERSON

ELLA'S LEGACY

BY

JOAN MILLS

They're just age-ivoried snapshots, dated May 20, 1926. Beside a backyard lilac, a dark-haired woman smiles at the infant in her arms. The baby returns the woman's look with a gaze of fascinated intensity. It appears that she is recording the moment to remember forever.

These are the first photographs of me, and the last of my mother's mother, Ella Frost. A few months before the gift of memory settled into me, my grandmother Ella died—resisting all the way. She was 53.

In my childhood, my parents' stories of Ella seemed but fancies made of mists, disconnected from the reality of *me*. We lived several years in what had been her house. When we moved on, mementos of Ella went with us: her gifted handiwork, old plates and pewter, some antique furniture.

Another cycle went round, and it became my own time of mourning—and choosing. Only when I had moved the most meaningful remembrances from my parents' house to mine did I realize that I'd let nothing of Ella's go. I'd been holding one of her cobalt-blue glass candlesticks to the light, for my soul's satisfaction at seeing such color. I knew that Ella had done the same thing, and had felt the same way. There was a pang in me then. We should have had more time to share, we two who had our hearts in the same place.

I couldn't have guessed that a day lay ahead when she would come directly into my life.

In the spring of 1972 my husband and I separated, preparatory to divorce. I was 46—a housewife, not a career woman. My only sure income was $20 a week for a homey little newspaper column. My other earnings were so chancy that I decided to live on a $3000 survival budget while I learned the ways of change. I needed perspective, a job, experience.

I became a full-time writer for the paper that carried my column. But I couldn't produce what was wanted. I tried. My editor sighed.

"I'm miserable," I confessed to my children. Dared I free-lance? I yearned to but my savings couldn't support the risk.

Brooding thus, I left the post office one day with an envelope from my Uncle Finley. Inside was a single page from the Springfield, Massachusetts, *Union,* where, when I was little, my dad had been a reporter and editor. Across the top, Finley had written: "Let's hope it's $100,000!" An inked line ran down through columns of names to *mine!* Reading further, I discovered that the Commonwealth had become the trustee of certain long-inactive bank accounts. Claimant could recover their assets via the probate court in Springfield.

My eyes popped. Was I rich?

Not likely. We'd moved from Springfield in 1935. I was nine, and the Depression was almost as old. This had to be my school savings; one shiny buffalo nickel a week, first grade through fourth! I went straight home and wrote the court an amusing account of my theory.

My claim was acknowledged. I'd guessed wrong. On October 4, 1928, Ella had opened an account in my name. That single deposit, plus 44 years of interest, would be delivered to me in court.

89

Ella? So near her end? With so little to spare, and life ebbing? The images rose of my grandmother and me, so taken with each other when my life was new. I felt as if, out of the shadows and across the years, a timely message had reached me: *I loved you then, I love you now.* Tears stung my eyes.

Waiting for my day in court, I tried to recollect everything I knew about Ella. Her family had emigrated from Germany to Springfield, where they established a small grocery. Ella was 19 when she married Bill Hickey, a handsome Irishman. At 23, a few weeks after my mother's first birthday, he died of tuberculosis. Ella, barely 21, resolved that neither she nor her baby would ever be the objects of pity.

Evenings she taught herself to sew exquisitely. For six years, with a sweet spirit, she raised her daughter alone. Then she married Harry Frost. They bought a little house in West Springfield. The neighbors were scandalized when Ella climbed on the roof in her highbutton shoes and petticoats to nail down new shingles. Tireless, she scraped paint, replastered walls, cut back the tangled shrubs, and then put in a garden of phlox, verbena and roses. She wove beautiful linens, even bedspreads and draperies. If a chair needed caning, she did that too. "My mother could do *anything!*" Mother used to say.

Ella had another baby then, a perfect little boy. When he was nine, Neil was killed in a street accident as Ella screamed. Once more she sewed into the night, healing herself in her own way. And, in time, when my parents lost their first baby, Ella comforted them. When I was born, she looked into my eyes and smiled.

She was already dying then—and, finally, she sank into protracted agony. Why did she never speak of her provision for me? I can only guess: to the last of her days, Ella meant to *live!*

Though it was just 50 miles distant, I hadn't been back to Springfield since childhood. I set out to claim my inheritance on a stormy winter day.

Cars were sliding helplessly off the turnpike; trucks crept along like a procession of timid ghosts. *Ghosts!* My mind was full of them.

An eager little girl, one I knew well, seemed to be sitting beside me. She guided us down a ramp and off the pike before I knew it had happened; then down a suddenly familiar road.

There's our house! And there's the church. Around that corner, I was born. Over the bridge and into the city. Did you think I had forgotten?

The courtroom was large and crowded. Mine was the first case called. Judge Abraham Smith leaned affably toward me as I approached the bench. "So!" he said, "you're the one who thought she'd be collecting her school savings!"

I laughed. "I am, Your Honor."

Smiling, he passed me a check. The figure astonished me: $2017.

Driving home, I was grateful for the hush of the snow and the slow pace of cars. I needed to think. More than ever, it seemed there was significance in my legacy.

It had come when I was alone, as once Ella had been. She'd had family then to give her courage. Unexpectedly, so now did I. Even the sum I'd just received seemed eerily intentional. Months before, I'd calculated that $2000 was the security I needed if I was to risk writing on my own, at home.

I thought about that. Such a life would always be precarious. *But I'm not expensive to keep,* I thought, brightening. Hadn't my grandmother made a rich life for herself and those around her with very little money? *I'll speak to my editor,* I decided. Beside me, where the child had been, I could almost see Ella—smiling.

Four weeks later I moved my typewriter into the living room. And I never had to draw on Ella's money. It wasn't that I prospered from the start—I lived very frugally. But the triumph of discovering that I could live debt-free by my own powers was a source of pride such as I'd never known.

My most meaningful legacy from Ella wasn't worldly wealth, but her example. In thinking about her, I had found my own strong center. It was my children, work, friendships and commitments that I valued. Life has so much good in it, if the heart perceives! I found blessings in lamplight and supper—and in laughter, where once I would have wept.

By the third year, my survival now secure, I felt a suspenseful stir of "What next?"

One of the oldest human needs is having someone to wonder where you are when you don't come home at night.

MARGARET MEAD

A lifetime of absorbing the lessons of ups and downs, calamity and repair, had made me an effective volunteer counselor at a community mental-health clinic. One of my mentors was a therapist of international reputation. He was taking his senior staff to London that spring, to lead some professional workshops.

"Now *that* would be an experience for you!" he said. "You'd learn a lot, and with all your training I think you'd be a contributor too."

I said yes—just like that, *yes!*

Was I the woman who, not long ago, had felt so unsure of so much?

Not now! To fly over the earth, to visit a city whose history and literature filled my imagination, seemed the perfect way to celebrate how far I'd come on my own journey. I'd stay on after the meetings, and make this the first great adventure of my life. *London!* Thus I spent Ella's legacy—gloriously.

It's a very affecting thing when dreams unfold past their usual season. I'd never bought an airline ticket before that one. When I picked up my passport, I couldn't read it for the tears of happiness.

My adventure was everything I'd wished upon, and more. One day, as I was walking near Buckingham Palace, a sudden jingle and clatter turned me about. Two open carriages, all gilt and crimson, were coming up the Mall. The first bore the Queen, the second, Prince Phillip; each with a state visitor.

Her Majesty was waving, and as her carriage swept by, our eyes met. I smiled. My eyes still on her, I nodded in mannerly acknowledgment, with the full composure of a self-realized, independent woman who could indeed go to London and see the Queen.

It was a delicious moment. Ella would have loved it.

STORIES ON A HEADBOARD

BY

ELAINE PONDANT

*T*he bed was about 45 years old when Mom passed it along to me a few months after my father died. I decided to strip the wood and refinish it for my daughter Melanie. The headboard was full of scratches.

Just before starting to take the paint off, I noticed that one of the scratches was a date: September 18, 1946, the day my parents were married. Then it struck me—this was the first bed they had as husband and wife!

Right above their wedding date was another name and date: "Elizabeth, October 22, 1947."

My mother answered the phone. "Who is Elizabeth," I asked, "and what does October 22, 1947, mean?"

"She's your sister."

I knew Mom had lost a baby, but I never saw this as anything more than a misfortune for my parents. After all, they went on to have five more children.

"You gave her a name?" I asked.

"Yes. Elizabeth has been watching us from heaven for 45 years. She's as much a part of me as any of you."

"Mom, there are a lot of dates and names I don't recognize on the headboard."

"June 8, 1959?" Mom asked.

"Yes. It says 'Sam.'"

"Sam was a black man who worked for your father at the plant. Your father was fair with everyone, treating those under him with equal respect, no matter what their race or religion. But there was a lot of racial tension at that time. There was also a union strike and a lot of trouble.

"One night some strikers surrounded your dad before he got to his car. Sam showed up with several friends, and the crowd dispersed. No one was hurt. The strike eventually ended, but your dad never forgot Sam. He said Sam was an answer to his prayer."

"Mom, there are other dates on the headboard. May I come over and talk to you about them?" I sensed the headboard was full of stories. I couldn't just strip and sand them away.

Over lunch, Mom told me about January 14, 1951, the day she lost her purse at the department store. Three days later, the purse arrived in the mail. A letter from a woman named Amy said: "I took $5 from your wallet to mail the purse to you. I hope you will understand." There was no return address, so Mom couldn't thank her, and there was nothing missing except the $5.

Then there was George. On December 15, 1967, George shot a rattlesnake poised to strike my brother Dominick. On September 18, 1971, my parents celebrated their silver wedding anniversary and renewed their vows.

I learned about a nurse named Janet who stayed by my mother and prayed with her after my sister Patricia's near-fatal fall from a swing.

There was a stranger who broke up the attempted mugging of my father but left without giving his name.

"Who is Ralph?" I asked.

"On February 18, 1966, Ralph saved your brother's life in Da Nang. Ralph was killed two years later on his second tour of duty."

My brother never spoke about the Vietnam War. The memories were deeply buried. My nephew's name is Ralph. Now I knew why.

"I almost stripped away these remarkable stories," I said. "How could you give this headboard to me?"

"Your dad and I carved our first date on the headboard the night we married. From then on, it was a diary of our life together. When Dad died, our life together was over. But the memories never die."

When I told my husband about the headboard, he said, "There's room for a lot more stories."

We moved the bed with the storybook headboard into our room. My husband and I have already carved in three dates and names: Barbara and Greg and Jackson. Someday, we'll tell Melanie the stories from her grandparents' lives and the stories from her parents' lives. And someday the bed will pass on to her.

Where Thou art—that—is Home.

EMILY DICKINSON

A MOTHER'S GUIDE
TO LIFE

BY

BARBARA TONER

*D*ear Daughters,

You are, as I've told you many times, the cleverest, wittiest, most ravishing girls who ever lived, and a constant source of heart-stopping pride. The other day, however, after too much coffee which made me hyperventilate, I got to worrying, "I have told them nothing." So I'm writing you this guide.

You may say, "But Mumma, we will learn the hard way, just as you did." My response is, "Why go my hard way when I now see the way round it?"

Owing to an impetuous nature and a sorry tendency to speak out of turn, my life has been full of blunders. My intention is to spare you what I can with the benefit of hindsight. Passing it on will make me feel a whole lot better about drinking too much coffee.

Inspirational Stuff. Life is a privilege and to waste it is sinful. You must accept responsibility for yourself, always use your talents to the best of your ability and contribute somehow to the common good.

The common good will present itself to you every day; a friend will want to talk endlessly about herself; an old lady will need help crossing the road and talk endlessly about herself (possibly me); your father will want his stapler back. Failure isn't not succeeding; it's not trying your hardest and not contributing, however modestly, to the common good.

Correct Thinking. What you need to meet life's challenges head-on is the right attitude. I mean, of course, not whining.

Hope for everything, but expect nothing. Know that anything can go wrong at any time and mostly does. You get your hair cut. You hope to look like Catherine Deneuve. You look like Danny DeVito. You think: *Aaargh!* Then you let go. Hair grows.

You hope to get a job. Some der-brain gets it. Correct thinking: it wasn't the job for me since I am not a der-brain. Soon I will get the job that is for me. Meanwhile I will work hard at a job which is beneath me just to show the kind of girl I am.

Assess, Attack, Accept. Say some boy dumps you. First, assess. There will be the usual possibilities: sobbing down the phone, getting friends to say you are on a life-support machine, sucking up to his mother. You may go for one or all of the options, or you may decide the situation is beyond hope and walk away from it. Whatever, you act on your decision and accept the outcome. Don't pine. Be miserable for a day or two, write a couple of sad poems, feel outraged and move on.

Whiners fail to act or accept. They say, "I can't" but mean "I won't."

Manners. You can say, "People should take me as they find me," but the real question is, "What do I want to be taken for?"

I want you to be taken for women who care at least a little about the comfort of others. This means having a bit of consideration. It means not shoveling your food, always saying please and thank you, watching your tongue and showing respect to everyone until they give you reason not to extend it. It means note-writing, phone calls or flowers to express thanks for hospitality, and offering to help clear the table and wash up.

There are manners for polite conversation: don't interrupt, don't speak across, don't hog the floor, don't be sullen. Never imagine you are being asked about yourself because you are interesting; you are being asked out of courtesy. You must show equal interest back.

This is how conversations should go: you ask about me; I ask about you; you tell a story; I tell a story; you venture an opinion; I venture mine; you comment on mine; I comment on yours. If someone says, "My cat's died," the correct response is not, "I don't have a cat."

Culture. Culture—a refined understanding of all things arty-farty—is somewhere between manners and education. You don't have to have it, but it's jolly nice if you do. To acquire it, you should travel widely, read widely, listen to and memorize music, go to concerts, operas, the theatre and art galleries. But frankly, who has the time or money?

Usually it's enough just to read the reviews, master a few foreign phrases and mix with informed people. Culture for most people is 70 percent bluffing, 25 percent genuine interest and 5 percent knowledge.

Money. Having grown up without any money, I have only modest respect for it. This has given your father heart failure on many occasions.

Don't be a wimp about money. Don't even try to kid yourself about your real financial situation. Draw a line down the center of a page and on one side total up what you are owed and on the other put outgoings yet to appear on the bank statement. You will notice that what you are owed is a very small column, while the other is a long one. This is normal.

If in serious debt, cut right back on your outgoings. It is disastrous for your mental health to build a debt you cannot repay.

On the other hand, there's nothing worse than a miser or a hoarder. If you are not impoverished, spend. Take the holiday, have the party, give the gift.

How to Be Successful. To get on in the world you must a) know what you want and b) decide how you are going to get it. I knew from the time I learned to read, when I was four, that I wanted to be a writer, and I have become one. But if your heart doesn't desire anything much, consult your head, which will consider your options in a detached and, with any luck, fruitful manner.

An employer wants intelligence without arrogance and confidence without brashness. Be prepared to start at the bottom and to endure months, possibly years, of humiliation and learning. Make yourself learn by asking questions. It's no big deal. We all did it.

In business, you will get more work the more people you please. What you must decide is how much of a compromise you are prepared to make. My advice is to be prepared to make endless compromises—there are, as your grandfather used to say, a hundred ways to skin a rabbit. But suggest the compromises yourself. Don't have them forced on you.

It's a mistake to imagine your job is what you are or that your success as a human being depends on great career moves. Learn to value yourself for what you are.

Sex, Love and Marriage. My advice would be to think ahead before you leap into bed with someone. You want affection and warmth as well as great sex, and you're not going to get that with a man whose interest in you is entirely physical. He will be entirely interested in himself. Forget him. You may definitely call me old-fashioned on this one.

Falling truly in love, as distinct from being unable to keep your hands off someone, is best achieved when there is enormous affection on both sides and a strong mental connection. Your father and I, for example, had a lot in common: we had similar family structures, were both in journalism and we made each other laugh, mostly in despair.

Even when you love someone, warts and all, there will be bones of contention on which one or the other of you, if not both, will balk at regular intervals—that is when mutual respect and acceptance can save you. They will be the governing factors long after desire has faded.

Your father and I are always going off on each other. He thinks I'm an arrogant, know-all cow and I think he's a grumbling, selectively deaf lunatic. But the perfect partner is one you can loathe and then learn to like again. Naturally there are times when we can't imagine living together another minute longer, but the minute passes. Then we can't imagine living apart.

The best final advice I can offer is that you live in the present. You can learn from the past and plan for the future, but get pleasure from the moment and give the moment your all. I don't think it will make you a better person. But it will make you happier and your lives richer.

Your ever-loving Mumma

> *Life affords no greater responsibility, no greater privilege, than the raising of the next generation.*
>
> C. EVERETT KOOP

You don't really understand human nature unless you know why a child on a merry-go-round will wave at his parents every time around—and why his parents will always wave back.

WILLIAM D. TAMMEUS

LETTERS
to EMMY

Special Feature

BY

GREG RAVER LAMPMAN

It was a question he hoped his daughter would never have to ask: "Whatever happened to Daddy?"

The thought chilled him. But it was a very real possibility. With an egg-shaped tumor lurking in his brain, Greg Raver Lampman well knew his days could be numbered.

So in a heroic and touching effort, he began his race against death, writing a series of sometimes hopeful, sometimes heartbreaking, but always touching letters to the little girl he might never see grow up.

Even if he lost the race, he could still reach beyond time and mortality with a father's message of love to his daughter.

Dear Emmy,

About two weeks ago, early in May, I remember reading you a story, then putting you to bed. Nothing unusual, until about three A.M. when the smoke alarm rang out. Mommy and I were both dead asleep. I scrambled out of bed, my heart pounding, fearing there was a fire. It turned out the batteries in the alarm were going bad. I took them out and climbed back into bed, but I couldn't calm myself. My heart was still pounding, making my head throb.

I fell asleep, but before daybreak I began to thrash around in bed. Mommy didn't understand what was going on at first. "Stop that," she kept saying. "It isn't funny."

The thrashing got worse. I was incoherent, flailing my arms and legs. That's when Mommy realized I was having a seizure.

She phoned the ambulance. When paramedics got to our house, I was slipping into unconsciousness. Mommy thought I was dying.

Slowly I seemed to emerge from the seizure. I sat on the edge of our bed, my eyes dilated, staring at the wall. *"Please,"* I pleaded in a frightened tone. *"Please."* The paramedics let me walk to our bathroom. There the convulsions hit again. I slammed onto the bathroom's tile floor with so much force that the impact fractured a vertebra in my back. Paramedics strapped me onto a gurney and took me to an ambulance.

This is where I had my first foggy memory of you. Emerging from a haze, I saw you, Emmy, in the ambulance, next to me. You were wearing your pink terry-cloth robe. You looked so frightened.

My next clear recollection is lying in bed in DePaul Medical Center in Norfolk, Virginia. I was in the emergency room, surrounded by a white curtain.

I remember seeing you again. You still had on your terry-cloth robe. You looked so dainty, so helpless. With your beautiful root-beer brown eyes, you stood staring at me strapped into a hospital bed. I ached to hold you.

As I became more aware, I complained about the pain in my back. A neurosurgeon, Dr. Jonathan Partington, ordered an MRI, a type of brain X ray that allows doctors to see inside your head. Partington believed the MRI might find out what caused the seizures.

About daybreak, Dr. Partington came by to visit me and Mommy. He was reassuring and wore gray tortoise-shell glasses that slid down his nose a bit. He hung up one of the MRI films and told us calmly and succinctly that I had a "common" brain tumor. I remember the comfort I took in the word *common*.

I could see the tumor on the piece of film. It was about the size of an egg, white and featureless, inside my skull. He told us the tumor was probably benign and explained the kind and shape of the cells that made it up. He told us everything a doctor should tell a patient, but all his explanations, all his talk, got swallowed up in one word: tumor. For Mommy and me, it spelled instant dread.

"What do we do now?" I asked.

The doctor said I had to be checked into the intensive-care unit. He would give me drugs to reduce the swelling in my brain. Then in several days, he would saw out a chunk of my skull and carve out the tumor. To be safe, he would have to slice some healthy brain tissue out too. I might lose some function on my right side or suffer problems with my speech, but the tumor had to come out. Even if it was benign, it would still eventually grow to the point where it would kill me.

After he left, Mommy and I struggled to take in what we had been told. Though we did not yet realize it, that polite little chat with the doctor would alter our lives dramatically. Over the next few days, as I waited for surgery, I tried to stay upbeat. I told all my visitors the same story. The tumor was benign. I'd survive. No need to worry. Mommy and I talked ourselves into expecting a few days in the hospital, a few months of recovery.

I still remember the morning of the operation. One moment I was on a surgical bed with Mommy standing nearby; the next, I was in intensive care, looking up at I.V. lines and heart monitors, breathing through a plastic oxygen mask. Mommy was holding my hand.

My mouth was dry from the anesthesia, so she gave me some ice chips. "I can move," I finally said, stretching out my words, and asked Mommy to kiss me.

Over the next few days, as I waited for surgery, I tried to stay upbeat.

A couple of days later, Dr. Partington showed up. He must have just come from another operation. I saw him clearly, leaning against the wall beyond the foot of my bed, wearing scrubs, looking tired, eating an ice cream bar.

In a relaxed tone he said that the hospital pathologist had examined my tumor removed during surgery. He thought that part of it was malignant. Mommy stood up next to my bed and took my hand.

The doctor went on. He wasn't sure he agreed with the diagnosis. He had seen the tumor during surgery, and it hadn't looked malignant to him. Sometimes, he explained, it could be difficult to make judgments. Mommy and I listened, dumbfounded.

Dr. Partington told us he had mailed samples of the tumor to the Armed Forces Institute of Pathology in Washington, D.C., to be examined by specialists there. They were "the best," he said.

When he left, I felt as if I'd betrayed you and Mommy. As Mommy cried, I thought, *How could I do this to her? Or to you?*

Like the Old Couple

Dear Emmy:

I remember the day I came back from the hospital, you ran into the living room shouting "Daddy! Daddy!" You were gentle. You didn't jump on the couch. At the hospital I had been fitted with a brace for my injured back. You kissed my cheek and snuggled into my arm. All you cared about was that your daddy was home. You just wanted to be near me.

At bedtime you asked me to read to you. I remember I read you the story about Elmer, the patchwork elephant. Those moments together were precious.

After I got my diagnosis, I had this urge to talk to you, to tell you what I've been feeling. But that's impossible. You're just three years old, living in a world of crayons and swings and sandboxes. How do you explain tumors and illness and death to a three-year-old?

So I decided to write down my thoughts and experiences, not just about my illness but about our life as a family. I saw these pages as being like those in a journal a father might keep for recording his toddler's growth; only this journal would record a time when both of us grew: you physically, me spiritually. I also wanted to reserve those moments of pure joy that I shared with you and Mommy.

One thing I want you to know, Emmy, is that Mommy and I always loved each other. For us, companionship goes back 16 years to the night we met in a bar and restaurant in Santa Cruz, California. Mommy had come there to dance. I've always been shy around women, but I didn't feel that way about Mommy. That first night she asked me to dance, and we spent hours talking about everything: travel, adventure, life, love, friendship.

Later, we started to live out the adventures we had talked about that night. One trip took us to Mexico. What I remember most was a ride through the Sonora desert aboard a slow-moving train. An old woman and an old man sat across from us on the wood-slat seats. So that the woman could recline, the old man—probably 80 years old—stood. The train had plenty of empty seats, but the man insisted on standing there, his hand lying gently on her shoulder. They looked so loving.

When we got married, Mommy had my wedding band engraved with these initials: FLTOC. *Forever Like the Old Couple.*

In the years since we met, love, travel and adventure seemed intertwined. After I graduated from college, we lived a year in Jamaica, another in Ecuador. Then I began working for a newspaper, and Mommy earned her doctorate. Seven years ago, a Virginia university hired her, and I got a job at a newspaper nearby. We bought a home, made good friends, started establishing roots.

We wanted someone else to share our love and our life. When we couldn't conceive a baby we decided to adopt. That's how you came into our lives. I remember those first moments holding you, Emmy. You were two months old. Even then you were spunky. You looked right at me with a goofy, toothless smile, and at that moment I felt love in its purest form.

Since then Mommy's worked at the university, I at the newspaper, often longer hours than I wanted. Some nights I didn't get home until you were asleep. Some weeks I'd see you only in the morning.

We had our adventures. When you were 21 months old, we spent several weeks in Wales, and now and then Mommy and I would dream of what we'd do in the future. Someday, she wanted to travel around the world. More immediately, we wanted to take a year off to teach in the Czech Republic. We always loved travel to places we had never been to before, and the Czech Republic was simply one of those foreign, exotic places we had promised ourselves we would visit.

Now those dreams have been replaced with the dread that not only are those dreams gone, but I may never see you graduate from high school or college; I may not be able to watch you grow up.

Even more, I worry about you watching me suffer. I know it was tough for you to see me so sick. During my first few days in the hospital, you were too frightened to sleep in your room. You slept with Mommy, holding her hand. And once when Grandma said she didn't feel well, you asked worriedly, "Are you going to fall down and shake like Daddy?"

To keep your mind off all this, Mommy signed you up for summer day camp and arranged to have you visit the homes of friends.

I remember how wonderful it was the first time you were to spend the night with two friends. You were so excited you jumped up and down, shouting, "I'm going to spend the night, I'm going to spend the night."

You ran downstairs and packed your pink backpack with toys and a special dress, as you called it. When your friends' parents pulled up in front of the house, you ran out the door. Without a look back at us, you walked right to the van, climbed inside, sat down, buckled your seat belt and waited.

"I *think* she's excited," I said to the other parents, who laughed.

Mommy gave you a quick kiss on the cheek. As you sat there, ready to give me a kiss, I asked, "Are you *sure* you want to go?"

"Yes, silly," you said. As the van pulled away, I have in my mind the image of your tiny hand waving to us through the van's back window.

Your first night sleeping at someone else's house—it was a milestone. One of the events parents include in a baby book. One of many in life.

I remember so well the first time you laughed. Mommy had bought a balloon for you and tied it to your crib. She knocked down the balloon, and as it floated back up you laughed out loud. When Mommy hit the balloon a second time, you started to laugh again so hard that Mommy and I began laughing uncontrollably along with you. Suddenly those moments have become all the more precious to me. They are the memories you and Mommy and I are creating together.

A New Battle

Dear Emmy:

After three days at home, our lives settled into a more regular pattern. Mommy took you to day camp in the morning on her way to work. That morning I got a call from Dr. Partington's office. He wanted to see us.

I called Mommy and she rushed home. We were nervous about being summoned so suddenly.

At the doctor's office we were escorted into a small examination room with a chair, a stool and an examining table covered with paper. I could hear Partington's muffled voice talking to a patient in another room. I wondered: *How can anyone have the presence to keep delivering so much bad news to others?*

You're going to die.

You're never going to walk again.

Partington's voice trailed off. Then he stepped inside our room, seeming relaxed and happy. "I figured you'd want to know as soon as I got word," Partington told us. Doctors at the Armed Forces Institute of Pathology had determined that my tumor was benign.

"That's great," I said. Now it seemed our worries were over. Then Dr. Partington suggested that I make an appointment for radiation treatment.

"But I don't understand. I thought it was benign," Mommy said.

"It is," Dr. Partington explained, "but these kinds of tumors—they're called astrocytomas—tend to come back." He went on to explain that if he had left anything behind, even one cell, the tumor would return. While radiation might not destroy all lingering cells, it would probably delay a recurrence.

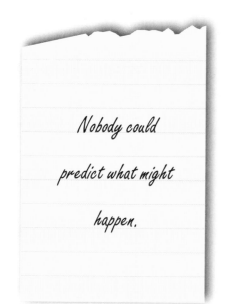

Nobody could predict what might happen.

We were confused. Radiation for a benign tumor wasn't something either of us had considered.

Mommy asked Partington about survival rates for untreated benign astrocytomas. At first Dr. Partington seemed reluctant to answer.

Even with benign astrocytomas, he said apologetically, patients have a high chance of recurrence.

Partington went on to explain that I had a lot going for me. The tumor had been removed; I had come out of surgery without obvious impairments. I was relatively young—37 years old—and there was promising research under way in biological and genetic medicine.

Nobody could predict what might happen, he repeated. But if I made it two years without any recurrence, my chance of surviving longer would improve a lot.

To this day I don't remember his exact words. Mommy had been staring blankly at the doctor, and then it hit her. Her face contorted as she tried to hold back the tears.

We told Dr. Partington we would have to think about the radiation treatment before we made a decision. The following weekend, I went to the Eastern Virginia Medical School library and searched for articles about my condition.

As I read them, I began to feel confused and sick. Some argued against radiation for benign tumors, because it either didn't seem to make much difference in survival or, in rare cases, it could cause severe neurological damage, leaving patients unable to work or take care of themselves.

The fact was, with or without radiation, people died. There were a few "long-term" survivors, but they were considered aberrations.

Over and over again the words all boiled down to the same thing: astrocytomas kill—most often in months. Increasingly I wondered: why undergo radiation, with its potential for complications, if I wouldn't live any longer?

"Don't Leave Me"

Dear Emmy:

My doctor recommended a radiation specialist, and Mommy and I went to see him. In his waiting room I looked around at the other patients. An older man sat down across from me with a big red square and a small "x" drawn on his neck in a special dye. To one side was an extremely gaunt man who looked exhausted.

"It's going to be okay," Mommy whispered as she held my hand.

A few moments after we walked in, the nurse led us into the doctor's examining room.

Looking over my chart, he talked as if radiation was already decided on. Mommy asked whether there would be side effects.

"Probably not much," he said, "other than hair loss."

"Will it grow back?" Mommy asked.

"Probably not," he said matter-of-factly.

Then he began to talk about starting treatments. Mommy and I interrupted at this point to tell him we hadn't decided on radiation therapy. He seemed surprised.

He admitted that a series of treatments applying intensive radiation to the brain usually was done only once because of the potentially catastrophic brain damage it could inflict. I asked about forgetting about the radiation and having Dr. Partington monitor my tumor.

"If it comes back, he could go in, cut out any new growth, and I could begin radiation then," I suggested. "That could still be a couple of years down the line."

"But this condition is curable," the specialist stressed.

From reading the medical papers, I'd already learned what "curable" meant to the experts. All it meant was that the patient survived five years without recurrence. What is five years? *In five years,* I thought, *you'll be just eight years old, Emmy.*

Ultimately, Mommy and I decided to get a third and final pathology report, just to confirm the diagnosis. We called Dr. Partington, who agreed to send my files to Memorial Sloan-Kettering Cancer Center in New York City for analysis, but he also warned us that delaying radiation could be risky.

He had just gotten the Army neuropathologist's final report. It identified my tumor as "low grade," or benign, but, ominously, it noted that it also had "atypical features." This suggested my tumor could be more aggressive than most. Still, we knew we wouldn't feel comfortable going ahead with the radiation until we heard back from Memorial Sloan-Kettering. So we decided to wait.

One morning, shortly after that visit, I sat on the couch feeling drained. Mommy came and sat next to me. She took my hands and looked into my eyes. I saw the eyes I remembered from so many years ago in Mexico, beautiful light brown eyes flecked with yellow.

Mommy's eyes glistened. "I love you so much," she told me.

"I love you too," I said.

"I don't want to be left alone," she said suddenly. "Please don't leave me alone."

It was like a knife to my heart. I wrapped my arms around her. I ached to tell her she never would be alone. But I knew I couldn't promise anything.

Too Late for Dreams

Dear Emmy:

You've been so sweet ever since I came home from the hospital. Sometimes you've treated me more like a patient than a daddy. But I know this illness is taking its toll on you. Last night, you dreamed the house fell down on top of you. In another nightmare, monsters came and took you to the hospital.

And for weeks you've been restless, waking well before sunrise. Mommy has exhausted herself trying to comfort you, trying to take care of me, and going to work. I know she has had as many sleepless nights as I have, as many worries, as many nightmares.

Because of my back injury, I haven't been able to get out of bed to pick you up, but I felt I needed to do something to help her get some rest. So last night, as you were getting ready for bed, I asked you to stay in your bed instead of jumping right up the next morning. I asked if you would try to read your books if you woke early.

The next morning, Mommy and I opened our eyes later than usual, feeling rested. It was probably the first full night's sleep Mommy'd had in weeks. As I sat up in bed, I heard the sound of paper rustling.

I got out of bed and went to your room to find you quietly sitting up in your bed, flipping through the pages of one of your books. You looked up at me and smiled.

"I'm reading my books, Daddy," you said. I felt so proud of you at that moment.

You and I were able to spend a good part of the day together. In the afternoon I started to wear down, so I made a snack—a "picnic," you called it—and we went upstairs to watch the movie *The Little Mermaid.*

You and I lay side by side on the bed, snacking and watching Ariel, the mermaid, fall in love with a human prince. As we watched the movie, we talked about the story.

"Someday," I whispered to you, "you're going to have a family of your own."

You looked at me, not understanding. "What do you mean?"

"You're going to have a family and children and a life of your own."

When I said that your eyes filled with tears. "But I'll *miss* you, Daddy. Stay with me when I get older."

That night after you and Mommy fell asleep, I stayed up, worrying. I had a clear sense my life was ending. I had always envisioned living to be an old man. Now, it seemed, I was on the final leg of my journey.

What drove me crazy was that the journey seemed so short. I'd put off so many hopes and dreams. I had always believed I'd have enough time. I had let too many of the less important things distract me and eat up my time. Now I wondered if it were suddenly too late.

I lay there next to Mommy in our dark room, watching TV, restlessly flipping channels, when I came across *The 700 Club,* Pat Robertson's evangelical news program. I flipped first to Jay Leno, then *Nightline,* but I couldn't focus.

As I flipped back through the channels, I saw Sheila Walsh, Pat Robertson's Scottish sidekick, talking. She said she understood that there are genuine tragedies in life. That tears and sorrow are real. That death is *real*.

Christ, she said, offers companionship. He is willing to stand at your side through sorrow. He understands. She opened the Bible and in her Scottish accent read the familiar Twenty-third Psalm: "...Though I walk through the valley of the shadow of death, I will fear no evil, for thou art with me."

I thought about the Psalm. There, in the dead of night, I found the idea so beautiful—companionship. I came to see how believing that someone will walk with you, that we don't die alone, that love endures, that someday, Emmy, we'll be together again, could be so comforting. And that night I felt at peace.

Long Wait

Dear Emmy:

Tonight Mommy went to see a friend, so at bedtime I read you a story called "Grandfather Twilight." As I left your room, you began to cry.

"Mommy didn't give me a kiss or a hug," you said.

"That's okay, Emmy," I told you. "I'll make sure she gives you a kiss when she gets home."

"No, I want a kiss now," you said.

"Mommy's not here," I said.

You continued to sob inconsolably.

"I'll give you an extra kiss and hug," I said.

"No," you said, "I want Mommy."

I didn't know what to do. You cried for about 15 minutes. I was exhausted and my back throbbed.

"Okay, Emmy," I said. You looked up at me with those brown eyes spilling tears. "I'll pretend to be Mommy."

I could see your look change, just a tad, as you pondered this strange idea.

"I'll pretend to be Mommy." I repeated, "and I'll give you a kiss and a hug, okay?"

You still looked slightly confused, then said cautiously, "Okay." I kissed you on the forehead and gave you a big hug.

In a few moments you were sound asleep. As I watched you lying there I thought how wonderful little moments like these had become for me and how life doesn't and shouldn't stop when you get sick.

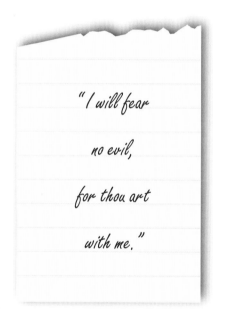

" I will fear

no evil,

for thou art

with me. "

A month passed since I had my surgery, and still no report from Memorial Sloan-Kettering in New York. I've felt, irrationally, that as long as nobody gives me that final diagnosis I can act as if everything's on hold. It is as though even my tumor is waiting for word from New York—which, of course, it isn't.

Mommy and I, I have realized, have become consumed by illness. Our house has become so cluttered with medicines and medical paraphernalia that our home itself seems "sick" to me.

That became ever clearer one morning when you were brushing your teeth. You and Mommy were in the bathroom. Mommy was quizzing you on our phone number and our address.

"And what number do you dial in an emergency?" Mommy asked.

"9-1-1," you recited. Then, after a moment, you added, "That's what you did when Daddy got sick."

"That's right," said Mommy.

I was tired of how my illness and concerns about my dying interfered with our normal life as a family. After I heard Mommy talking to you, I decided it was time we made a real effort to get on with living. So we went to the zoo. This was our first outing together since my return home. Even though I wore my back brace and a hat to cover my shaved head and my scar, I felt like a father again.

When we got home, Mommy cooked a fancy meal, and we all sat in the dining room. After dinner I washed the dishes while you went out to play in your new sandbox.

A few days later I went with Mommy to pick you up at day camp. All three of us went out for ice cream. When we got home, I remembered a kite with a blue unicorn on it that we bought before I was sick. You and I went out to a small park nearby to fly it.

The day was warm and windy. Neighborhood kids played soccer and football nearby. Your kite jumped up and snapped in the breeze hundreds of yards above us. Your joy seemed so complete as you held the string of your kite and watched it cut through the china-blue sky.

As we stood there in the warm breeze, I thought about how friends and relatives remained obsessed with the Memorial Sloan-Kettering pathology report.

"Why is it taking so long?" one of my sisters asked.

"As far as I'm concerned, no news is good news," I told her.

Nobody seems to understand that I'm really not looking forward to getting the report. As long as it remains in New York, I'm free from making any hard decisions, and free to cherish the silence.

And silence means I can just go on living, free to enjoy flying a kite with you, Emmy, free to imagine that these days with you will stretch out forever.

Happy Interlude

Dear Emmy:

On July 9, about two months after I returned from the hospital, Mommy and I celebrated our thirteenth wedding anniversary. It was 16 years ago that Mommy and I met in California. Sixteen years since we traveled through Mexico together.

When Mommy woke up that morning, she found you and me huddled on the couch together.

"I want Daddy to dress me," you told Mommy.

"Okay, but I'll do your hair," Mommy said.

"I want Daddy to do my hair."

"Emmy…" Mommy began.

"Please, please, please, please…"

Mommy gave in.

You and I went upstairs. You'd already laid out a dress the night before. I helped you put it on and was lacing up your shoes when I realized that I hadn't dressed you since my seizure. I braided your hair and put in a bow decorated with a cluster of deflated balloons.

Mommy was taking you off to swimming lessons and day camp. "Happy anniversary," Mommy said to me lovingly before she left.

"Happy anniversary," I whispered and gave her a long hug.

On her way out the door, Mommy reminded me to check on the pathology report. She was annoyed we hadn't heard anything from Memorial Sloan-Kettering.

"If it was bad, I don't think they'd take this long," I replied. "They're probably waiting to type it up."

But she insisted. *Call Dr. Partington.*

That morning I called Dr. Partington. I told him my wife was nervous. I told him I didn't want the whole report; I just needed to confirm that the tumor was in fact benign. For her, I said. Partington told me he was leaving on a two-week vacation soon and said he'd try to get the report before he left.

I hung up the phone with a sinking feeling. *What if this tumor's not benign? But of course,* I told myself, *it is.* I knew it in my gut. The fact that it could be another week or two before I heard brought me down, but then I reminded myself it was our *anniversary*. I knew how much Mommy loved anniversaries, and I wanted this one to be special.

We planned to go out to dinner and celebrate the wonderful years we'd already had and forget about illness for just this one night.

That night during our "date," Mommy and I talked and laughed and kissed. We remembered the wonderful times we'd shared. We talked about how excited we were the night before your adoption and recalled the day we drove home from the adoption agency with you in our front seat, our third musketeer.

The next morning after you and Mommy left for the day, Dr. Partington called. He'd finally received a preliminary pathology report.

The Memorial Sloan-Kettering specialist said my tumor was malignant. I was stunned. "Well," I said, struggling for words, "what do we do now?"

Of course, his answer was radiation. He suggested I get started immediately. "You know," he reminded me, "my recommendation always was radiation."

I told him I understood. I had gambled and I had lost. Nonetheless, I was angry. Over the last two months I'd adjusted to living with a benign tumor. The original seizures had been like a trapdoor opening. I'd finally come to feel that I had regained my balance. This new pathology report was like another trapdoor opening. I was in free fall again.

Still, I didn't have time to wallow in my depression. I knew I had to get my appointments and insurance authorizations lined up. Within two hours, I had a week of medical meetings scheduled.

Before long I heard our pickup truck pull into the driveway. You and Mommy and a little friend, Kate, got out. You'd been excited all week about bringing her home. "Daddy!" you shouted as you ran in and hugged my leg.

Mommy went to the dining room where she was distracted with putting her purse and papers away and looking through the day's mail. After you and Kate ran outside, she asked whether I had a good day. I stood there dumbly. I didn't know what to say.

"What's wrong?" she asked. In those seconds, I could see realization dawning in her eyes.

"The pathology report?" she asked.

When I still couldn't say anything, she knew.

I walked toward her. We stood in the living room, our arms wrapped around each other while you and your friend played on the swing.

Love Forever

Dear Emmy:

Mommy and I had planned to take you to a water park near Williamsburg, an hour from our home. With the new pathology report, Mommy thought we ought to cancel the plans. Somehow, that seemed wrong to me. Not going would be giving in to my illness. "Let's enjoy the weekend," I told Mommy.

On the drive you snuggled between Mommy and me in the front seat. As you slept, Mommy and I talked about everything.

I had told you that we were going to the water park as part of our decision to "celebrate" every moment. This obviously made a big impression on you. As we walked around, you got a cup and started talking into it, enjoying the echo. You pretended it was a telephone and began talking in a robotic voice.

"You-and-Mommy-are-going-to-celebrate," you intoned. "That's-all-you-ever-do. Celebrate-celebrate-celebrate." Mommy and I laughed.

I took the cup and said in a mechanical voice. "Do-you-know-why-we-celebrate?"

You took the cup. "Because," you said, "you-love-the-world."

At the water park, you spent most of your time in the kids' section, going down slides, walking under umbrella waterfalls. At one point, you coaxed me into an inner tube in the kids' pool and then shoved it under a waterfall, laughing long and hard. You've always had this great, booming laugh. It was a wonderful sound.

The following morning you woke up cranky, and as you were leaving for camp you inexplicably came over to hug my leg.

"Are you happy or sad?" I asked.

"A little bit happy," you said, "and a little bit sad."

"Why are you sad?" I asked

You looked up at me with your big eyes. "Because you're going to be sick again."

Later that day when Mommy went to pick you up, you were more upset. As she buckled your seat belt you threw a ferocious tantrum. With both anger and terror you declared "*Daddy's* going to the *hospital*."

Mommy was surprised but didn't want to lie to you. "Yes," she said calmly, "Daddy's going to the hospital."

At that, you started to sob. Mommy couldn't do anything to comfort you.

It was shortly after that I remembered the locket. Mommy has a tiny, gold, heart-shaped locket. Inside are our pictures, taken soon after we met. You've always loved that locket, loved opening it to look at our pictures. I once told you this was Mommy's special locket.

"Will you buy me a special locket?" you asked.

"Yes, when you turn 13," I promised. You've never forgotten that promise.

Since I wasn't sure I'd be around to give it to you, I decided to buy one now. Mommy and I drove to a jewelry store.

"May I help you?" asked the woman behind the counter.

I tried to answer, but I felt choked up and walked away. As I came back to the counter, one locket stood out among all others. It was gold and heart-shaped, with pink- and green-tinged filigree. I could picture you wearing it on your thirteenth birthday. "Let's get that one," I said. "Inscribe it, 'Love forever, Daddy.'"

The Battle Begins

Dear Emmy:

Mommy and I were caught up in medical chores today, running back and forth to the hospital. You must have sensed the tension as we ran around, fielding phone calls, virtually ignoring you.

And you must have felt frightened. At one point, you called me, saying, "Daddy, I have a surprise."

At first I ignored you as I talked on the phone, trying to signal for you to be quiet.

"Daddy," you said again, "I have a surprise."

"Please, Emmy, just a minute," I said as I covered the receiver.

For a few minutes, you waited patiently, then said, "Daddy, I *have a surprise.*" When I finished that phone call, I rushed upstairs to see your "surprise."

"Close your eyes, Daddy," you commanded when I got to the door of your room. You took my hand and guided me inside.

"You can open now," you said. I opened my eyes to see that you had meticulously cleaned your room. You'd lined all your stuffed animals along your pillow. You'd put away every one of your crayons. You'd even made your bed, pulling the comforter over the pillows. You had never cleaned your room before.

"Emmy," I said, surprised and touched. "It looks beautiful."

You stood there beaming with pride. I bent down and wrapped my arms around you in a long warm hug. That's what you'd been needing all along.

At the hospital the doctors told me my latest MRI revealed that I have a blood clot the size of a thumbnail in my brain. I had a CT scan to determine its density and whether "it's something we may want to evacuate." Meaning more brain surgery.

In the end, my doctors decided to wait on the surgery and begin radiation treatment immediately. The risk of further delay outweighed the risk that the clot might grow.

The first step in my radiation was the mark-up. I lay on a hard, flat table while an array of lasers shone from different directions on my head, creating a crosshatch of light beams. Then a nurse got a bottle of dye and painted over the lines. I lay there, smelling the ink, feeling the cold brush strokes, wondering what I would look like.

I lay there...wondering what I would look like.

When I walked out, with the painted lines still on my head, I looked toward the receptionist.

"Well?" I asked.

"Your daughter's going to think you have war paint on," she said, smiling. I looked around the waiting room and could see people staring at me. The red crosses lining my head made me look as if I'd joined some strange cult.

Later that night, as I put you to bed, I showed you the red lines. You thought they were neat. You rubbed the stubble on top of my head where I had been shaved from my brain surgery. "Your hair's coming back," you said.

"I know," I told you. "But soon I'm going to be totally bald." I tried to say it as cheerfully as possible.

"Your whole head will be *bald*?"

"Yes," I said. "And every night, you can rub it."

"I don't want your whole head to be bald. It's going to look funny," you said seriously. "People are going to laugh."

The first radiation session wasn't too different from the mark-up. Two technicians escorted me into a room with a linear accelerator, a monstrous device that looked like an oversized X-ray machine. They rotated the linear accelerator to a target point near my left temple.

Both technicians left through a huge metallic door. Then I heard the static hum of the accelerator generating power. Seconds later, the device made a brief buzzing noise. I lay perfectly still, wondering what might happen to my brain as the accelerator fired the radiation into my left temple.

According to my doctors, over the course of the treatment series my brain will be blasted with radiation strong enough to kill the cancer—along with swaths of brain cells nearby.

A few days later I went to lunch with some friends at the newspaper. I looked at them and saw myself three months ago. I remember I used to hear a siren, or see an ambulance, and wonder whether there was some story I should chase. Now, when I hear a siren, my first reaction is a pang of empathy, of fear that someone may be suffering. *Let them be okay,* I think.

"Magic" Daddy

Dear Emmy:

This afternoon, you, Mommy and I headed for King's Dominion, an amusement park about three hours from here. When we arrived, you went wild, going on every ride. I was grateful to be watching you.

Today I realized, Emmy, I've grown to know you so much better because of the illness. When I worked at the newspaper, I attempted to have what I told myself was "quality time" with you. Now it seems that was just a lame attempt to cram parenthood into short blocks of time. Since I've been recuperating, I've spent hours of unhurried time with you and we've become so much closer. Could I have gotten to know you this well if I'd remained healthy? I don't think so.

At one point, you ran over to a game where people win stuffed animals by shooting a water gun at a target. I've never done well at games like that.

"Daddy, could you win me a surprise?" you asked.

"I don't think so," I told you. "If I play, it doesn't mean I'll win."

"Please?"

So we stood and watched other people playing. Whenever somebody won, you turned to me again.

"Daddy, win me a surprise," you said.

When I hesitated you suddenly burst into tears. A woman behind the counter leaned over and whispered something to you.

"I want my daddy to *win* me a surprise," you told her, sobbing. I could tell this wasn't a phony cry; you seemed genuinely hurt. Even the woman at the counter was touched. She reached under the counter and pulled out a stuffed alligator. "Here you go," she said.

You took the alligator and thanked her. But as we walked away, you handed the toy to Mommy. "Don't you like the alligator?" she asked.

You shrugged. Then it was clear to me. It wasn't that you wanted a stuffed animal; you wanted me to *win* you something.

I sat down at a horse-race game, in which you advanced the horse by shooting at a target. I had horse No. 14 and was competing against a dozen people.

"If you don't win," Mommy said, "you're going to break her heart."

"I know," I said. "But I've got to try."

I concentrated only on aiming at the target and shot without watching the horse. I heard a lot of commotion, then a bell.

"Number 14," the carny said.

"Daddy won!" you shouted.

I couldn't believe it. I'd never won anything like that before.

You picked out a colorful stuffed clown. "Clowny," you called him. You were so proud. You carried Clowny with you the rest of the day. You walked up to another girl, showed her Clowny and said, "My daddy *won* this for me."

For you, today, your daddy was magic.

Graduation Promise

Dear Emmy:

I quickly settle into the pattern that will govern my life for the next month. Every morning at 9:15, Mommy takes me to the hospital for treatment, which lasts ten minutes or so.

On Monday, doctors also check my blood, to make sure the radiation isn't depressing my immune system too much. On Tuesday, the therapists tape diodes—radiation sensors—to my hair to check the strength of the radiation. On Friday, I meet with a radiation specialist.

Today Mommy took me for my daily radiation treatment. As I walked in, I heard the nurse at the front desk congratulating a woman who was "graduating," meaning she'd finished her treatments. I got a kick out of that.

"When I graduate," I joked to Mommy, "I want to have a graduation party."

"It's a deal," she said.

It's begun. For weeks now I've been psyching myself up for the hair loss from radiation therapy. After my treatment one morning, as I was reading a book, I noticed three or four hairs drift down onto the page. I brushed them aside. Then a few more fell.

I reached up and tugged on a hair. It came out, almost like pulling weeds—no feeling. I lightly tugged at a wad of hair on top of my head and it came out as if it had never been attached. I felt nauseated.

I tried to go back to reading, but I couldn't stop thinking about my hair. I ran my fingers through my hair and more fell out.

By the next day it had fallen out clean to the scalp on one side. "I look like a freak, don't I?" I said to Mommy.

"Noooo," she said. We looked at each other, and I started to feel lousy. Mommy understood exactly how I felt because she looked at me lovingly. "It's the pits, isn't it?" she said.

That night I tossed and turned, and when I couldn't fall asleep I walked around the house, worried.

I went back to bed but sill couldn't sleep. Finally I drifted of to a fitful sleep at maybe five o'clock. Soon after, I heard you. You walked over and stood next to our bed. I knew I should send you back to your room. But I opened up the blankets and you crawled in. I drifted off, feeling comfortable, sleeping a deep, dreamless sleep.

A Great Day

Dear Emmy:

My brother Doug flew in from California a couple of nights ago. Throughout this ordeal, I have been in regular contact with my family. I've talked to Doug, my mom and my three sisters on the phone dozens of times, keeping them posted. But I hadn't seen any of them since my surgery.

I drifted off, feeling comfortable, sleeping a deep, dreamless sleep.

Mommy and I stood in the corridor of the airport, and I wondered how Doug would react. Finally, we saw him at the end of the hallway, coming toward us. Doug is one year younger than I am, and he looked good. And his hair was so *thick,* I couldn't help but think. He waved when he saw us.

Doug seemed surprised that I appeared as healthy as I did. I guess he was expecting to find me strapped in some hospital bed. I remember, just before he flew out, he said: "If you have any surprises, tell me now. I want to know about it before I get to the airport."

He did seem a bit put off by my bald head, which was by now quite blistered from the radiation.

After Doug arrived, we had a couple of lazy days. He decided he wanted to go hang gliding on the sand dunes of Kitty Hawk, North Carolina. I knew I couldn't hang glide because of my back. But I thought: *What the hell? I can watch.*

We headed for Kitty Hawk. An afternoon storm cleared just as Doug and I started to walk up the dunes for his first flight. The view from the ridge was spectacular. Layers of white, billowy clouds and thunderheads floated along the horizon. Down below in a sandy valley a dozen people swam in a pond formed by the storm.

As we reached the top of the dune, I looked down to see you running toward me. You'd never seen anything like this before. It probably looked like a giant sandbox with people hanging from kites.

For two hours, as the sun set slowly behind the layers of clouds, we watched Doug soar. He would glide down the hill and over the beach, sometimes skimming only a few feet above the sand. I loved it. It made me feel alive. At dusk, I took you to the pond where you peeled off your clothes and paddled around in your underwear.

Then we all checked into our motel. You and Mommy were tired, but Doug wanted to go to a local nightclub, and I went with him. He ordered a drink and I had a soda because I couldn't have alcohol with my medications. Pretty soon he ordered another round and was enjoying himself, chatting with the waitresses, even exchanging wisecracks with the comedian on the stage.

When we left, he gave me the keys to the car because he had been drinking. Although I wasn't supposed to drive because of my seizure, we both figured it would probably be safer with me behind the wheel than him. As we pulled up in front of the motel, Doug noticed a small tavern across the street and suggested we go in.

Inside, a guy with a guitar was singing old Beatles songs. Doug noticed that next to him was an unused electric keyboard.

"Hey," Doug said, "my brother plays keyboard. He could jam along." He turned to me. "Go for it."

"Nah," I said. "No way."

So Doug went to the keyboard while the guy with the guitar sang. Doug started banging away even though he doesn't play.

Unable to contain myself, I went up, pushed him aside and started playing along with the guitarist, watching his fingers to figure out the chords. Doug left the stage and walked over to a woman at the bar and asked her to dance. They moved in front of the stage, doing a kind of swing dance as I played.

"That's great," Doug shouted.

For the next two hours, I played.

It was well after one A.M. when Doug said he was ready to leave. Once outside, we walked smack into a North Carolina squall. The rain came down so hard it bounced off the pavement.

We ran toward our motel, but we were getting so wet Doug ducked into a covered bus shelter. When I joined him, we stood there awkwardly.

I don't know if it's true for all brothers, but for Doug and me talking can be tough. As we stood soaking wet under the shelter, I knew we were both thinking about *it*—my illness. I had shoved it aside all day. Now, in the dark, I could feel it there, hanging between us.

"Man," Doug said, "you were great."

I didn't say anything.

"I mean it," Doug said.

He seemed to be struggling to say something. "I mean, *no matter what,*" he went on, emphasizing each word, *"this was a great day."*

He was right. It was a great day. A crazy-great day. The kind of day you remember. The kind of day you laugh about years later. It was living. It was being brothers.

There were no cars on the street. We lapsed into silence again.

"I heard you might have six years," he said out of the blue.

"Yeah, maybe. Nobody really knows."

"Yeah, but . . . " He seemed desperate and sad at the same time. "I mean you're just the *same*. All the girls were wondering, 'What's he going to be like?'"

I could picture them, my sisters, wondering what Doug would find. Wondering what had happened to their big brother.

"And you're *okay*," Doug said, and there was something in his voice that was heartbreaking. Then he put his arm around me, and we stood silently watching the rain.

Savor the Day

As we walked out of the house, I was struck by how beautiful the night was.

Dear Emmy:

Shortly before Doug flew home, I had an MRI to see what had happened to the blood clot in my brain.

When Dr. Partington walked into the room, he seemed cheerful. "Have you seen your MRI?" he asked. He beckoned us to a hallway where it hung on a wall of flourescent light. "This is where the tumor was debulked," he said, pointing to a black cavity in the brain. "This," he said, pointing to a bright white line surrounding the cavity, "looks like normal scar tissue."

I felt a huge sense of relief. The clot no longer existed, which meant there would be no surgery. Even better, there was no evidence that the tumor had returned.

During all earlier visits, he had made it clear that the tumor would return at some point. He always talked about operating.

Now he began talking about what we'd do "when the tumor comes back, if ever."

As we walked across the parking lot, I turned to Mommy. "*If ever*, he said. *If ever*. He never said that before."

"I know," she said. "Maybe you'll be one of those rare cures."

We got into the car and drove home. In the car, Mommy began to cry with relief.

It was clear and cool, one of the nicest days we'd had since Doug arrived. As we drove home, I watched other people in the cars all around us, people heading to and from work, doing chores. I sat in the passenger's seat and thought about those two words: *If ever*.

And now, I have only one more radiation treatment. I'm going to walk in Monday, get my treatment, and walk out. And it will be over.

With the radiation complete, I'll begin to get my life in order again. But for this weekend I decided just to relax. I hung around the house, playing piano, writing, talking to friends on the phone.

That afternoon, Emmy, we walked to the 7-Eleven, just you and I. You had gotten to love those trips. We wandered around and when we felt like it, we made detours.

During this trip, I took your kite with us. A storm was developing as we walked. Wind gusted from every direction. When I felt a gust, I threw your kite into the air. It shot up, tethered by a short string, sometimes circling around you as the wind changed. We spent probably an hour walking, flying the kite, sitting, talking. The afternoon was magical. By the time we got home, a tremendous thunderstorm had rolled in. "Get some rest," Mommy told me as the storm raged outside. We were going out to eat that night, so I went upstairs and took a nap. I woke feeling rested for the first time in a week.

By then the storm had cleared. As we walked out of the house, I was struck by how beautiful the night was. The clouds looked magnificent, a mishmash of white and gray, illuminated by the moon.

"Let's walk," I said.

I felt exhilarated. As we walked, fresh, cold rainwater dripped from the trees onto my bare arms. We ducked under rain-soaked myrtle branches. I brushed soggy pink flowers from the brim of my hat.

At that moment I had no notion how my life was going to turn out. But I was determined at least to savor the day.

When we walked into the restaurant, Mommy told the host we had reservations.

I could see empty tables all over the place. I thought, *Reservations? You don't need reservations tonight.*

Then, as we walked farther into the dining room, I saw a long table with a group of about 30 people. I saw someone I recognized from the newspaper. Damn, I thought. I figured this was some newspaper group out for an evening meeting the same night we were dining.

Then I saw some of our neighbors at the table and friends and people from church who had brought me food over the past four months. This gathering didn't make any sense. What were these people doing together? What was the connection?

Then it dawned on me. I was the connection. This was arranged. Mommy did this. I was too stunned to act surprised.

This was my graduation party.

A "Lifetime" Ahead

Dear Emmy:

It's December, winter now. Three months have passed since that sweltering August day when I had my very last radiation treatment. Just a few days later, you celebrated your fourth birthday. I was grateful for the fact that I had enough energy to tie balloons, cut the cake, take photographs and sing "Happy Birthday."

Two months after my last treatment I flew to California to visit Doug, my mother and my sisters. I had spoken to them on the phone dozens of times, but it couldn't compare to being with them, staying up late talking, remembering, laughing.

After avoiding doctors and hospitals for three months, it was tough returning for my first follow-up MRI to detect any new tumor growth.

Today, Mommy and I went to Dr. Partington's office to get the results of the MRI. It was perfect, Partington said. As far as he could tell, my tumor was gone, for now. He gave me a physical exam and I had another pleasant surprise: my hair had slowly begun to grow back.

Mommy and I walked from his office holding hands and taking in the rich, wonderful world around us. I couldn't wait to get home and hold you in my arms.

The clouds have passed, at least for another three months. I've begun to dare to look a little further ahead. Now, I can consider truly being a part of your life, Emmy. And now I can look forward to the day I place that gold locket around your neck, on your thirteenth birthday.

Over these seven months, I've grown vividly aware that in life there are no extra days or second chances. Like many of my friends, I used to feel comfortable sacrificing today, tomorrow, a week, maybe a year, in hopes of something better in the future. Now I sense how wasted moments and wasted hours get woven into wasted lives.

Obviously, I would have preferred never to have had the tumor, but because of it I have learned a hard and important lesson: you have to live deliberately. By that, Emmy, I mean you can't just sleepwalk through life hoping that *someday* you'll get around to doing what you really want to do, that *someday* you'll realize your dreams. Living always has to start from now.

And above all, don't be afraid to dream your dreams. You need dreams to look forward to; without them your soul will wither away.

I don't know how much time I have remaining. But, I have learned this: short or long, it's a lifetime. My lifetime. To be lived.

From the loving example of one family a
whole state becomes loving.

THE GREAT LEARNING

MIKE AND ME
AND THE CAKE

BY

MICHAEL A. ANDREWS

Our nine-year-old son, Mike, came home from his Cub Scout meeting to tell us his pack would be hosting a banquet and cake sale. The cakes were to be baked by the Cub Scout and his father.

I'd never baked a cake. But, having seen my wife use instant mixes, I looked forward to the project without undue consternation.

When the day came, Mike and I selected a yellow instant cake mix. Following instructions, we mixed the ingredients and poured the batter into two round pans. Confidently we placed the pans in the oven. Taking them out after 30 minutes, in strict accordance with the instructions, I was surprised that the cakes were not the tall and fluffy ones I'd seen in ads. In fact, they only half filled the pans. Mike didn't seem to notice, and besides, I told him, some of the best cakes I'd ever eaten had been shortcakes.

We stacked one cake upon the other, and I then learned that confectioners' sugar was needed to make the frosting. We had no confectioners' sugar. We also had no time. The banquet was only an hour away.

I wasn't even sure what confectioners' sugar was. Well, sugar is sugar, I reasoned. But my wife gently persuaded me that regular granulated

138

sugar was entirely unacceptable. I made a frantic trip to the supermarket and returned with a can of ready-made frosting.

We were already late for the banquet as we scraped and smoothed the frosting over the cake. We got it all looking frosted, even if it was a bit thin in spots. As a finishing touch I made decorative little dabs on top, inspired, I suppose, by the rough-textured paint on our kitchen ceiling. Mike and I traded grins of accomplishment. We thought it looked good.

My wife laughed. Then she said it was sweet and looked just fine. I hadn't noticed that it sloped down on one side. As we hurried to the banquet, Mike casually mentioned that the cake sale would be an auction. For a moment I wished we'd had a little more time for finishing touches.

The hall was filled with people. Dinner was in progress, so we took our cake to the auction room.

I was stunned. A long table was filled with a fantastic array of exquisitely designed masterpieces—angel-food, devil's-food, spice, carrot, pound—all exotically iced and imaginatively festooned. Perhaps Mike had misunderstood and this was some kind of world cake competition. Perhaps the fathers and sons could have been assisted by mothers, professional decorators and engineers. Perhaps we were in the wrong place.

There were cakes shaped like Indian teepees, rocket ships, Scout emblems, hats, the United States, people and animals. There were toppings of cherries and glazes, marshmallows and candy glitter. Cakes were displayed on ornate cake pans and porcelain serving dishes. There were cakes topped with ornaments—miniature flags, figures of Cub Scouts, *Star Wars* battle scenes, and landscapes.

Mike solemnly carried our cake forward, on the same paper plate on which we had frosted it. Seeing there was no room alongside the others, he placed it on a radiator behind the table. Carefully, almost reverently,

he unwrapped the aluminum foil covering it. Frosting stuck to the foil in several spots, revealing blotches of yellow cake. I felt a flush coming to my face as I watched Mike. But he didn't seem to be ashamed of our creation.

I decided to suggest that perhaps we shouldn't participate in this auction, that perhaps . . . But those thoughts were interrupted by a deafening roar as a torrent of little blue uniforms poured into the room.

I couldn't hear the rules. A matronly den mother relayed portions of them to me as her toddler climbed my right leg. Only the Scouts could be in the auction area and bid. I hurriedly gave Mike eight dollars and, as he rushed back to where the cakes were, I shouted at him to bid low, to get the most he could for his money.

After five minutes of little boys screaming at one another to be quiet, the ordeal began. The auctioneer raised the first cake. He described its design, the intricate ornamentation, the exotic fillings, the bright colors and the cherry topping. He suggested those attributes warranted a high opening bid. "Seventy-five cents! Eighty cents! One dollar! Going once, twice; sold for one dollar." The next cake was described and sold for 50 cents. I anticipated the audience reaction to our cake and felt a dull pain inside.

My son would probably pretend he didn't know our cake when its time came. I could almost hear the boos and groans.

I tried to make signals to him across the room. I desperately mulled the idea of somehow moving forward and accidentally bumping our cake for the purpose of destroying it, thereby sparing Mike the impending humiliation. *Son, buy a cake—any cake—and let's leave,* I thought. Then the woman beside me began watching me suspiciously. I gave up.

Was it my imagination, or was the auctioneer tactfully avoiding our cake? I began to overhear people in the audience murmuring about the one with the "yellow blotches." Some teenagers behind me called it the Leprosy Cake and laughed. My heart ached for Mike.

The moment arrived. The auctioneer raised our cake. The paper plate sagged over his hand. Crumbs fell off. The numerous holes in the frosting shone garishly beneath the bright overhead lights. He opened his mouth to speak. But before he could utter a sound, Mike was on his feet, yelling at the top of his lungs, "Eight dollars!"

There was a stunned silence. No counterbids were offered. After a couple of double takes, the auctioneer quietly said, "Well, okay . . ." Mike ran forward, wearing a wall-to-wall grin. I heard him tell friends en route: "That's my cake! My dad and I made that cake!"

He handed over the eight dollars and beamed at the cake as if it were a treasure. Smiling, he worked his way through the crowd, stopping once to sample the frosting with a deft swoop of his index finger. When he saw me, he shouted, "Dad, I got it!"

We drove home happy, Mike holding his prize on his lap. I asked why he'd opened the bidding by offering all the money he had, and he answered, "I didn't want anyone else to get our cake!"

"Our cake." It was *our* cake. But I had seen it only through my eyes— not those of that special little boy who is my son. Once we got home, we each had a piece of *our* cake before Mike went to bed. It tasted pretty good. And, by golly, it looked rather nice too.

THE DAY MOTHER CRIED

BY
GERALD MOORE

Coming home from school that dark winter's day so long ago, I was filled with anticipation. I had a new issue of my favorite sports magazine tucked under my arm, and the house to myself. Dad was at work, my sister was away, and Mother wouldn't be home from her new job for an hour. I bounded up the steps, burst into the living room and flipped on a light.

I was shocked into stillness by what I saw. Mother, pulled into a tight ball with her face in her hands, sat at the far end of the couch. She was crying. I had never seen her cry.

I approached cautiously and touched her shoulder. "Mother?" I said. "What's happened?"

She took a long breath and managed a weak smile. "It's nothing, really. Nothing important. Just that I'm going to lose this new job. I can't type fast enough."

"But you've only been there three days," I said. "You'll catch on." I was repeating a line she had spoken to me a hundred times when I was having trouble learning or doing something important to me. "No," she said sadly. "There's no time for that. I can't carry my end of the load. I'm making everyone in the office work twice as hard."

"They're just giving you too much work," I said, hoping to find injustice where she saw failure. She was too honest to accept that.

"I always said I could do anything I set my mind to," she said. "And I still think I can in most things. But I can't do this."

I felt helpless and out of place. At age 16 I still assumed Mother could do anything. Some years before, when we sold our ranch and moved to town, Mother had decided to open a day nursery. She had no training, but that didn't stand in her way. She sent away for correspondence courses in child care, did the lessons and in six months formally qualified herself for the task. It wasn't long before she had a full enrollment and a waiting list. Parents praised her, and the children proved by their reluctance to leave in the afternoon that she had won their affection. I accepted all this as a perfectly normal instance of Mother's ability.

But neither the nursery nor the motel my parents bought later had provided enough income to send my sister and me to college. I was a high-school sophomore when we sold the motel. In two years I would be ready for college. In three more my sister would want to go. Time was running out, and Mother was frantic for ways to save money. It was clear that Dad could do no more than he was doing already—farming 80 acres in addition to holding a full-time job.

Looking back, I sometimes wonder how much help I deserved. Like many kids of 16, I wanted my parents' time and attention, but it never occurred to me that they might have needs and problems of their own. In fact, I understood nothing of their own lives because I looked only at my own.

A few months after we'd sold the motel, Mother arrived home with a used typewriter. It skipped between certain letters and the keyboard was soft. At dinner that night I pronounced the machine a "piece of junk."

"That's all we can afford," Mother said. "It's good enough to learn on." And from that day on, as soon as the table was cleared and the dishes were done, Mother would disappear into her sewing room to practice. The slow tap, tap, tap went on some nights until midnight.

It was nearly Christmas when I heard her tell Dad one night that a good job was available at the radio station. "It would be such interesting work," she said. "But this typing isn't coming along very fast."

"If you want the job, go ask for it," Dad encouraged her.

I was not the least bit surprised, or impressed, when Mother got the job. But she was ecstatic.

Monday, after her first day at work, I could see that the excitement was gone. Mother looked tired and drawn. I responded by ignoring her.

Tuesday, Dad made dinner and cleaned the kitchen. Mother stayed in her sewing room, practicing. "Is Mother all right?" I asked Dad.

"She's having a little trouble with her typing," he said. "She needs to practice. I think she'd appreciate it if we all helped out a bit more."

"I already do a lot," I said, immediately on guard.

"I know you do," Dad said evenly. "And you may have to do more. You might just remember that she is working primarily so you can go to college."

I honestly didn't care. In a pique I called a friend and went out to get a soda. When I came home the house was dark, except for the band of light showing under Mother's door. It seemed to me that her typing had got even slower. I wished she would just forget the whole thing.

My shock and embarrassment at finding Mother in tears on Wednesday was a perfect index of how little I understood the pressures on her. Sitting beside her on the couch, I began very slowly to understand.

"I guess we all have to fail sometime," Mother said quietly. I could sense her pain and the tension of holding back the strong emotions that were interrupted by my arrival. Suddenly, something inside me turned. I reached out and put my arms around her.

She broke then. She put her face against my shoulder and sobbed. I held her close and didn't try to talk. I knew I was doing what I should, what I could, and that it was enough. In that moment, feeling Mother's back racked with emotion, I understood for the first time her vulnerability. She was still my mother, but she was something more: a person like me, capable of fear and hurt and failure. I could feel her pain as she must have felt mine on a thousand occasions when I had sought comfort in her arms.

Then it was over. Wiping away the tears, Mother stood and faced me. "Well, son, I may be a slow typist, but I'm not a parasite and I won't keep a job I can't do. I'm going to ask tomorrow if I can finish out the week. Then I'll resign."

And that's what she did. Her boss apologized to her, saying that he had underestimated his workload as badly as she had overestimated her typing ability. They parted with mutual respect, he offering a week's pay and she refusing it. A week later Mother took a job selling dry goods at half the salary the radio station had offered. "It's a job I can do," she said simply. But the evening practice sessions on the old green typewriter continued. I had a very different feeling now when I passed her door at night and heard her tapping away. I knew there was something more going on in there than a woman learning to type.

When I left for college two years later, Mother had an office job with better pay and more responsibility. I have to believe that in some strange way she learned as much from her moment of defeat as I did, because several years later, when I had finished school and proudly accepted a job as a newspaper reporter, she had already been a reporter with our hometown paper for six months.

Mother and I never spoke again about the afternoon when she broke down. But more than once, when I failed on a first attempt and was tempted by pride of frustration to scrap something I truly wanted, I would remember her selling dresses while she learned to type. In seeing her weakness I had not only learned to appreciate her strengths, I had discovered some of my own.

Not long ago, I helped Mother celebrate her sixty-second birthday. I made dinner for my parents and cleaned up the kitchen afterward. Mother came in to visit while I worked, and I was reminded of the day years before when she had come home with that terrible old typewriter. "By the way," I said. "Whatever happened to that monster typewriter?"

"Oh, I still have it," she said. "It's a memento, you know . . . of the day you realized your mother was human. Things are a lot easier when people know you're human."

I had never guessed that she saw what happened to me that day. I laughed at myself. "Someday," I said, "I wish you would give me that machine."

"I will," she said, "but on one condition."

"What's that?"

"That you never have it fixed. It is nearly impossible to type on that machine and that's the way it served this family best."

I smiled at the thought. "And another thing," she said. "Never put off hugging someone when you feel like it. You may miss the chance forever."

I put my arms around her and hugged her and felt a deep gratitude for that moment, for all the moments of joy she had given me over the years. "Happy birthday!" I said.

The old green typewriter sits in my office now, unrepaired. It *is* a memento, but what it recalls for me is not quite what it recalled for Mother. When I'm having trouble with a story and think about giving

This is courage in a man: to bear unflinchingly what heaven sends.

EURIPIDES

up, or when I start to feel sorry for myself and think things should be easier for me, I roll a piece of paper into that cranky old machine and type, word by painful word, just the way Mother did. What I remember then is not her failure, but her courage, the courage to go ahead.

It's the best memento anyone ever gave me.

THE FAMILY THAT WOULDN'T BE BROKEN

BY

JOHN PEKKANEN

*S*oon after the birth of his son, Steven, Lindy Kunishima gathered his daughters, Trudi, 13, and Jennifer, nine, in the living room of their Honolulu home.

"I want to tell you a story," the American-born descendant of Japanese samurai said. "One day a samurai warrior sat down with his three sons and took out an arrow. He asked each son to break it. All of them broke it easily. Then he took three arrows, all bound together, and placed them before his sons. 'Now break these three arrows,' he said. None of them could do it."

As he neared the end of this story, Lindy gazed steadily into his daughters' eyes. "Then the samurai turned to his sons and said, 'That is your lesson. If you three stick together, you will never be defeated.'"

As the only boy in Lindy and Geri Kunishima's close-knit family, Steven occupied an honored place. His two sisters doted on him from the day he was born in September 1982.

When Steven reached six months, however, his mother grew concerned. Schoolteacher Geri Kunishima couldn't understand why her son still woke up crying several times every night to be fed. His daytime behavior was also puzzling. Steven would stay wherever Geri put him, seldom moving or making a noise. "He's not like the girls were at this age," Geri told her pediatrician.

"You're overanxious," he said. "Steven is doing just fine. Little girls tend to develop faster."

At 18 months, Steven still could not walk or talk, and early in 1984 Geri took her son to a neurologist. A CT scan revealed that the vermis, an area of the brain that transmits messages to and from the body's muscles, had not developed.

This condition—called bypoplasia of the vermis—explained why Steven's muscles remained soft and flaccid. It also explained why he woke up so often at night—his tongue muscles were too weak for him to swallow enough milk to satisfy his hunger.

"Mrs. Kunishima," the neurologist said, "I'm afraid your son will never walk or talk, or do much of anything else that requires muscle control."

Struggling to get a grip on herself, Geri asked how this would affect Steven's intelligence. "He will be profoundly retarded," the doctor replied, "uneducable for all but the simplest task. At some future time, you might consider putting him into an institution."

Shattered by the diagnosis, she couldn't eat or sleep for days. Late at night, Trudi and Jennifer could hear their mother's muffled sobbing and the gentle words of their father, trying to console her.

Jennifer, now 11, was also struggling with her emotions. She was a top student and a natural athlete with a wide circle of friends. Although she loved Steven deeply, she couldn't cope with her friends' knowing she had a brother who was not perfect. So, around them, she avoided any mention of Steven.

Trudi was also a top student and an achiever. However, at 15 she had the wisdom of someone older than her years. She was more able to accept Steven's handicap—and yet she wondered how disabled he really was. One day, trying to ease her mother's sadness, Trudi challenged the doctor's prognosis. "Mom," she announced, "I just don't believe what he said about Steven. Jen and I see a spark in his eyes. You can't give up on him. He won't have a chance if you do."

Trudi's words forced Geri to summon her fighting spirit. She called a family council around the kitchen table.

"I've thought about what Trudi said to me today," Geri began. "When the two of you were little, your father and I read to you a lot. We felt it would stimulate your minds and help teach you language. I think we should do the same for Steven."

"Yes!" Trudi agreed excitedly.

"We won't miss a night," Jennifer promised.

The four joined hands across the table and bowed their heads. "From this moment," Geri said, "we pledge to do everything in our power to help Steven."

The next evening, as Geri prepared dinner, Trudi unfolded a small futon on the white-tiled kitchen floor and propped her brother upright on cushions. She cradled his head in her arms because he couldn't hold it up for long and, snuggling next to him, began to read from a children's book.

Another reading followed the next night—and the next, until it became a half-hour ritual every dinnertime. Along with reading, Jennifer and Trudi asked questions and pointed out animals or people illustrated in the books. But week after week Steven only kept staring blankly into space, seemingly lost in a dark, empty world. *He's not even looking at the pictures,* Geri thought. *Will we ever unlock what's in this child?*

Gradually, Geri felt despair winning again. One morning in the predawn stillness of their bedroom, she poured out her feelings to Lindy.

"The girls are trying everything," she said, "but nothing registers with Steven. I don't even know whether the reading is helping or hurting."

"We may never be sure," Lindy conceded. "But in my heart, I know doing something is better then doing nothing."

"Time for reading, Steven," Trudi announced, nestling with her brother on the kitchen floor. After three months, he had still shown no response. He seldom even moved. That evening, however, he suddenly wriggled away from the cushions.

"Look at Steven!" Trudi called to her mother. In stunned surprise, they watched as he dragged himself across the floor. Inching to the children's books along the wall, he pawed at one.

"What's he doing?" Trudi asked.

Unable to turn the pages with his fingers, Steven whacked through the book with his hands. When he came to a page filled with pictures of animals, he gazed at it for a long time. Then, just as quickly as it opened, Steven's world shut down again.

The following night, the scene was repeated. As Jennifer prepared to read, her brother crawled to the same book and pawed it open to the same page. Speechless, the two sisters gave him a hug, laughing and crying at the same time.

"Steven's got a memory!" Geri marveled.

By now, Geri was on leave of absence from her job so she could devote more time to her son. As the months passed, Steven showed more and more response to the nightly reading. From her study of the subject, Geri learned that other parts of the brain can often compensate when one area is damaged. *Maybe that's happening with Steven,* she thought.

Both Trudi and Jennifer played the piano, and now they propped Steven under the grand piano while they played. One day after practic-

The greatest gifts you can give your children are the roots of responsibility and the wings of independence.

DENIS WAITLEY

151

ing, Jennifer lifted Steven from his place under the piano. This time, he was uttering a new sound. "He's humming the music he just heard!" Jennifer shouted to her parents. "Steven," she said, "you understand music, don't you?" The boy broke into a smile.

At the same time, the family also worked to build up his muscles. Lindy attended a massage school and learned how to knead his son's  arms and legs. Geri, Trudi and Jennifer dabbed peanut butter on the boy's lips. By licking it off, he exercised his tongue and jaw. They also gave him gum to chew and feathers to blow. Slowly, flaccid muscles in Steven's face began to strengthen.

When Steven was 4 1/2 years old, he still couldn't speak words, but he could make "aaah" and "waaah" sounds. Also, with a walker, he could now stand and take slow, shuffling steps. Moreover, he displayed a surprising visual memory. After studying the picture on a 300-piece jigsaw puzzle, he could assemble the pieces in one sitting.

Still, Steven was rejected by every preschool his mother applied to. Finally she took him to Louise Bogart, then director of the L. Robert Allen Montessori School at Honolulu's Chaminade University.

Bogart watched as Steven crawled on her office floor. He lifted his head, trying to speak to his mother. "Aaaah . . . aaaaah," he repeated again and again, gesturing insistently. Bogart saw the pain and frustration in his face. But she also saw something else: Steven was determined to make himself understood.

"Mrs. Kunishima," Bogart said, "we would be happy to have Steven in our school."

In the months that followed, the boy continued making slow progress. One morning, in his second year at Montessori, he was playing idly with blocks on a mat. Bogart stood off to the side, watching the teacher work with another child on numbers.

"What number comes next?" the teacher asked.

The child drew a blank.

"Twenty!" Steven blurted.

Bogart's head swiveled. Steven had not only spoken clearly but also given the correct answer.

Bogart approached the teacher. "Did Steven ever work on this?" she asked.

"No," the teacher answered. "We worked with him a lot on numbers one through ten, but we didn't know he had learned any beyond ten."

When Geri picked Steven up after school, Bogart told her what had happened. "This is just the beginning of what he's capable of," Bogart said.

Jennifer felt a knot in her stomach as her father drove her to her first high-school basketball game one night in February 1990. Steven, now seven, sat silently in the back seat, watching the passing traffic.

Jennifer's love for her brother was as strong as ever, but she still tried to keep his disability a secret. And that was becoming more difficult. Two years before, Steven had learned to speak, and his speech revealed his problem. "Please Dad," Jennifer whispered before heading to the locker room, "try to keep Steven from yelling during the game."

When the game started, Steven became caught up in the excitement. "Come on, Jennifer!" He shouted in his slow and halting speech. Jennifer cringed in embarrassment and refused to look at her brother. She knew she was letting him down; she was not being the strong third arrow. But she could not help herself.

At home, however, Jennifer lavished affection and attention on her brother. His motor skills remained poor, so Jennifer, Geri and Trudi worked hard at making his written scrawl legible. "I can do it," Steven assured Jennifer one day. "Just give me time."

For Steven, the biggest challenge of all was simply getting around. One typical morning, Geri heard a thud from the kitchen. "He's fallen again," Geri said, rushing to her son's side.

By now, Steven had fallen so many times that his knees were crisscrossed with scars. Yet Steven never cried when he fell. He even developed a sense of humor about it. Once, wearing slippers when he tumbled, he turned to his parents, eyes dancing. "Now I know why they call these slippers," he said.

"I really need to go to this camp," Jennifer told her high-school principal one day in March 1991. "It's very important to me."

Camp Paumalu, located 25 miles north of Honolulu, was held twice a year for four days to help students meet challenges, develop leadership skills and confront their fears and problems. Jennifer had begun to realize that a major obstacle was the torment she felt about mentioning Steven to her friends.

At the camp one afternoon, as she walked on the grounds talking with a boy from her high school, Jennifer felt her problem boiling to the surface, and words poured forth. "I have a brother," she told the boy. "I was never mean to him, but in a sense I was. I never wanted to face the fact that he has a disability. I always wanted to pretend it would go away." When Jennifer finally finished, she sensed the burden lifting.

On the last day of camp, each student wrote the fear or problem to be overcome on a pine board. Then the camper ceremonially broke the board with a chop of the hand or foot, symbolically breaking through the obstacle. On her board, Jennifer printed out her problem in large letters. Then she slammed her hand downward, but not until her fifth try was there a resounding crack as the wood splintered in two.

The next day, arriving home, Jennifer threw both arms around her mother, "I'm free, Mom," she said. "I'm finally free."

Jennifer's acceptance of Steven was now total. That fall, at her first basketball game of the season, she again heard Steven's loud voice cheering her on. Turning toward her brother, she waved to him eagerly. *Now,* her father thought, *the three arrows are truly bound together.*

For three years, beginning in 1990, Steven attended Holy Trinity School, a mainstream Catholic school. Learning still came hard, but Steven's speech and writing had improved to normal, and his physical movement was close to normal. By age 11, he was working at grade-level for his age. He could run and jump, and—like Jennifer—started playing basketball.

In 1992, Steven came to the attention of Lynne Waihee, wife of Hawaiian Gov. John Waihee. Hawaii's first lady had chaired a "Read to Me" program that encouraged people to read to children. Impressed by how much reading had helped Steven, she arranged for the Governor's Council for Literacy to honor the Kunishimas.

In a reception at the governor's mansion, Geri introduced Steven, who told more than 200 area leaders of his struggles over the years. He received a standing ovation.

In March 1993, the Hawaiian chapter of the American Red Cross presented Lynne Waihee its 1993 Humanitarian Award. She asked Steven to write a dedication for her awards-banquet program. For hours, Steven pondered what to say. Finally, he summed up what reading meant to him, and in so doing he spelled out the triumph of the Kunishima family. "Reading is important," Steven wrote. "My family reads to me and now I can read to myself."

The strength of a nation derives from the integrity of the home.

CONFUCIUS

MY UNFORGETTABLE PAPA

BY

RODELLO HUNTER

I remember Papa best standing behind the fence that surrounded our home, one huge, sun-browned hand resting on the topmost board. My father had carved his initials into that board on the very day it was nailed in place—a cause for punishment at the time. But now those initials were precious to Papa, and he often rubbed his fingers over them unconsciously as he waited by the fence for me to come home from school.

Papa wasn't my father. He was my paternal grandfather. His name was David William Hicken. He lived the first eighty-seven years of his life in Heber City, Utah—"in the most beautiful valley in the world," as he often said. His wife for 59 years was Mama Kate, and she was the "most beautiful" in the world too. "Kate," he told her when she was nearing eighty, "you've got the best lookin' legs of any woman in the valley."

My grandparents adopted me when I was seven. My father was dead, and my mother had remarried. By the time I went to live with them, Mama and Papa were in their late sixties, and Mama was showing the wear of many years. She was frail and sometimes forgetful, calling me by the names of her daughters grown and gone. But Papa was sinewy and strong, his hair only touched with white, his mustache dark and luxuriant, his purple-blue eyes sparkling with enthusiasm for "all that God has wrought," which, he told me, included the circumstances of my living with him. Ray and I (Ray was the son of Mama's sister, who had died in childbirth) were the last of the twelve children Papa and Mama reared—seven of their own and five "borrowed."

I remember in particular one afternoon when I was hurrying home from school, trying to keep a few feet ahead of Cynthia Thomas, who lived up the street. She was a pale, thin creature, one of those unfortunates always shunted aside by the most exuberant children. I saw Papa waiting for me at the gate, and waved, but he did not wave back. He met me with a stern face. "Why weren't you walking with the Thomas girl?" he asked.

"Oh, Papa, nobody likes her. If you play with her, nobody'll play with you. She's so . . . so . . . *you* know."

"No," he said. "I don't know. But I do know that I never thought I'd be ashamed of one of my daughters, and to this day I never have been. But I am now!"

In our family prayers that night, Papa asked the Lord "to humble Rodello's proud heart and give her the gift of gratitude for the privilege of living in this beautiful world in harmony with all other good souls." Thereafter I walked with Cynthia. And in all the years since that night I have often found myself mentally pausing to wait for some "good soul." I didn't want Papa to be ashamed of me again.

Sometime in his youth, Papa had made a friend of work. A full day's work done gave him a good night's rest and zest for the morrow. He was a high priest in the Mormon Church, and the church filled all of his leisure time. Rather, it was the other way about. After the church came his life's work—farming. He loved God first, then his family, and then

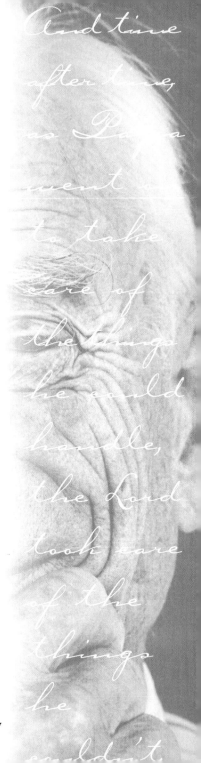

157

his neighbor as himself. And that neighbor didn't have to be a Mormon, either. In fact, I think he would have preferred non-Mormons, for then he would have the joy of converting them.

It was his "great faith" that people most often mentioned when they spoke of him. When the burdens (and I was one of them) grew too much for him, he would say to the Lord, "Father, I've done all I can, and it's too much for me. I'm going to have to put it in Your hands." And time after time, as Papa went on to take care of the things he could handle, the Lord took care of the things he couldn't. There may be some who will scoff at the simplicity, but as Papa said so often, "What you see, you know!" We all saw.

We saw, rather than heard about, honesty in Papa's house. He didn't "hold with sharp business practices"—no matter how legal they were. When little pigs were selling for $8 each, Papa charged $2 for ours "because no weeny pig in this world is worth more than that, and it'd be dishonest to charge more." Dishonesty was shorting your employer of one minute of a day's work. Papa thought that "cigareets" were inventions of the Devil at least in part because a man couldn't do any work while he was "suckin' on a cig."

But Papa could be exasperating at times, too. The minimum electric bill from our municipally operated power plant was $1 a month. It was a matter of principle with Papa that our bill never go over that. In the midst of my greatly anticipated "Lux Radio Theater" program, Papa would march into the living room and snap off the radio. "We don't have money to pay for such trash," he'd say. "Such trash" included novels, magazine stories and, later, TV (although he liked news broadcasts, and was an avid boxing fan).

Other than poetry, I don't think Papa could have brought himself to read anything written by a woman. He didn't believe women could think as well as men, and education past high school for his daughters was something he never considered.

But he loved us. Oh, how he loved us. He wanted us to marry husbands who "were men enough to wash dishes or change diapers if ever the need should arise," and he judged a very different, distant sort of son-in-law to be a good man "the day I saw him put those two babes of his in the tub and bathe them as gently as their mother."

Papa had a way of making everyday things important. At any gathering of note, he was generally asked to dance "The Man in the Flying Trapeze." This was always the hit of the evening—not because he was good, mind you, but because he really believed he was. His dancing was something between a shuffle and an early Wright brothers' takeoff, but people enjoyed him so much they actually cheered. Even now when you visit Heber City and ask about David Hicken, there will be someone who will tell you of his wonderful dancing—and they, too, will believe that it was wonderful.

Papa was past forty when he was made marshal of Heber City, an appointment which never brought him more than $75 a month. While he was marshal, there was a telephone in the house, because it was necessary. But the day after he left office he had it removed because we could no longer afford the extravagance. He was a formidable lawman, even though he never learned to shoot his revolver. Every morning he asked for the Lord's protection, expected it, and walked absolutely without fear. When Uncle Dave Hicken said, "Git," troublemakers got!

But after the guilty had been punished, the slate was wiped clean as far as Papa was concerned, and the offender was invited home to dinner. Everyone who stayed in Papa's jail was fed at our table before he was released.

When the Great Depression came, we had no money. But Papa owned his farm and house, and he raised a garden that covered half a city block. We canned the produce from the garden, and what we didn't can and couldn't eat, Papa gave away. I've gone with him trip after trip as he left sacks of potatoes, carrots, corn, pumpkins and other garden produce on the porches of the widowed, the orphaned and the ill. He gave because he found pleasure in giving. We welcomed people into our house because they were "our sisters and brothers."

We welcomed a lot of sisters and brothers during those lean years. Ours was a gate the homeless and hungry found with ease, and I was frequently asked to give up my bed to a stranger, or warned to "small down on the rice pudding" while our guest was urged to second helpings. There was one young man, named Robert, who stayed with us more than a month, until the woodpile was all chopped and stacked, the granary cleaned out, the fall plowing done. And then he left. Mama cried. "Poor boy," she said. "I don't know what I'd do if it was one of mine out there never knowing where he'd get his next meal." (Robert's next six meals were in a sugar sack slung over his shoulder; his shirt and overcoat were Papa's.) More than a year later Robert wrote and said that he found a job, and thanked us for "saving his life." And with that letter Papa and Mama were more than repaid.

One freezing February morning, when Papa was seventy-two, the doctor came and took him to the hospital for surgery. For almost two years after that he couldn't walk and was confined to bed. We set up a hospital bed in the front room, and from there Papa ruled the household much as he always had. For me, those two years were the richest time of my growing up. When I came home from school my grandfather greeted me happily and insisted that I sit beside his bed to do my lessons. He was deeply interested in the happenings of my school day, what I had done, whom I had seen on the long walk home. Everything.

One evening, at Papa's request, we had a family concert. Papa played the flute, Mama the Jew's-harp, Ray the drums, and I the piano. I

Family faces are

magic mirrors.

GAIL LUMET BUCKLEY

thought we were wonderful. We played "The Girl I Left Behind Me," "When It's Springtime in the Rockies," and "When Johnny Comes Marching Home."

Our first concert was such a success that we began to repeat it several times a week. We sang, too, so often that if I choose I can still shut my ears to the sounds of the world and hear the echoes of Papa's clear, strong baritone. When we sang, we would sit in the dark, with only the flickering of the wood stove to light the room. After the concerts, Mama served vinegar candy (you stretch it like taffy) or buttered popcorn, or hot chocolate with a dollop of rich cream on top.

I never knew that we were living in a Great Depression, or that hospital bills and bank closings had wiped out Papa's lifesavings, or that we sang in the dark to save on the light bill. As long as Papa laughed and sang, we laughed and sang, too, and the worst of the Depression slipped behind us. "I don't know how we ever made it through that awful time," I heard him say to Mama in the years afterward. But I knew. Papa led us through, playing on his flute.

After a couple of years of not walking, Papa got better, and before long he was up on a ladder painting the house. Mama died when he was eighty-four, and the eight years between her death and his own were long ones for Papa. Three of them he spent alone in the old house, and then he sadly fastened his gate for the last time and came to live with me in Salt Lake City. So we had come full circle. Now it was I who pulled the covers up to his chin at night and placed a glass of water on the table beside his bed. Once again we exchanged information, and he offered bits of his hard-found wisdom.

"Your child will forgive you easily and love you always if you punish him when he has done wrong," he told me. "But he will never forgive you, and perhaps never love you, if you do *not* punish him when he has done wrong." On another night—"Now, girl, you can only ask of life what you are willing to give it—so it's to your advantage to give it all you can." I will always treasure his last bit of wry praise. "You know, you are not at all bad to talk to—for a woman."

Papa was one of the world's good men. I adored him as a child, appreciated him even as a condescending teenager, loved him with a maternal compassion in his last years. But to my great remorse, I never once told him so.

Oh, Papa, you knew so much without being told. I hope you knew how much I loved you!

Who takes the child by the hand, takes the
mother by the heart.

DANISH PROVERB

GOING HOME ALONE

BY

PAMELA LANSDEN

As I boarded the plane for my flight home to Los Angeles from New York, I was pleased to see I might have two seats all to myself. Exhausted and grateful for the extra room, I buckled my seat belt and nodded off.

I was entering a state of semicoma when, just before our departure, I looked up and saw the flight attendant and a small blond blur clutching a fluorescent green-and-blue knapsack. He registered briefly in my consciousness as a Macaulay Culkin type. *Oh great*, I groaned to myself. *I bet he's a brat.* He climbed over me, took the seat and turned to the window. I went back to sleep.

The flight was well under way as I came to and saw that my seatmate was watching me wake up. I introduced myself and made the routine inquiries kids suffer through. Age: eight. Grade: third. I asked if his parents were on board. "No."

Suddenly his big, blue-gray eyes were locked on mine, forbidding me to turn away. His expression was strangely stiff, and I realized he was trying to control the muscles in his face. The harder he tried to hold his chin up, the more it quivered.

"What's wrong?" I asked. By then tears were no secret between us. His watery gaze unbroken, he answered my question with the rawest, most emotionally naked statement I've ever heard: "I want my mommy."

The boy had said good-bye to his mother at Kennedy Airport and was en route to his father, who had custody of him. "I just miss her so much," he said as his little chest quaked with each sob. "She cried too," he told me, as though to defend his outpouring of emotion by putting himself in the best of all possible company. This explained the youngster's late entry on the plane and conjured up a parting too painful to dwell on.

"This is ridiculous. I can't cry the whole five hours," he said, interrupting the sobs that had interrupted his telling me how he and his mom had stayed up late, taken taxis, seen a movie, shopped at F.A.O. Schwarz and blown the money his dad had given him. Putting on a brave face, he tried to talk of other things; but he kept coming back to the realization that the plane was carrying him farther and farther from his mom. "I just wish she were here," he kept saying.

I asked if he could tell his dad how he felt.

"He'd just say, 'Why do you care?' He doesn't even like her," the boy said. "I miss her a lot, but I can't go on crying," he continued, wiping his eyes with the wet sleeve of his sweater.

Clumsily, I offered him the few truths I have learned about turbulent times: life can be really hard. And you'll always feel better after you've felt bad. But I didn't know how to tell him there are no ready palliatives for the sweet sorrows of good-byes.

This child is one of the many who travel solo from one home to another, the lost luggage of parents who couldn't stand each other and now have to divide their offspring between them. Perhaps it's not fair of

me to question the domestic arrangements of others. Yet, as I listened to the heart of this eight-year-old, I couldn't help but wonder if these parents might have tried harder had they seen his pain. And I remembered how the notion of "staying together for the kids' sake" had been laughed off the face of the marital map by the time I was the boy's age and growing up in a broken home.

Maybe two adults bowing to someone smaller and something larger than themselves wasn't such a bad idea after all. Sitting next to my new friend, I thought it made a lot of sense.

A child on a farm sees a plane fly overhead

and dreams of a faraway place. A traveler on

the plane sees the farmhouse . . . and

dreams of home.

CARL BURNS

MY FATHER'S FINAL GIFT

BY
JOAN CETRANGELO CURTIS

Whenever my father came through the front door of our house in High Point, North Carolina, his rich, resonant laugh rose in an operatic crescendo. My two sisters and I would run through the dining room and leap into his arms. His classic Roman face would break into a smile as bright as the Mediterranean sun, and his sea-green eyes would sparkle with pleasure. He brought music and joy into our lives.

My mother's practical, disciplined Yankee upbringing couldn't have prepared her for the man she chose to marry. His moods traveled up and down like the tides. He moved his hands like windmills, his expressive face changed with every emotion, and his voice rose and fell with excitement or sadness.

When happy, he soared, telling stories, laughing or singing. But his unhappiness brought gloom to the household, which draped itself in mourning and waited for the return of his laughter. Often he was mischievous, and loved to tease our long-suffering mother. If she got angry, he'd make everything better with a kiss or a song.

Every evening after dinner he strummed his mandolin and serenaded us with tunes like *"O Sole Mio."* My father's family crossed the Atlantic when he was three, and he grew up loving Italian music. He told us stories about the great opera singers, especially the incomparable Enrico Caruso.

After my sisters and I went upstairs to bed, my mother played the piano and they sang. My father's rich baritone blended with the slightly off-key sounds coming from my mother while they sang popular tunes like "Who's Sorry Now" and "My Buddy." We drifted off to sleep in the harmony and assurance of their love. Their music wrapped around me like strong, secure arms.

My father, an artist who hand-painted furniture, had his own business subcontracting for local furniture companies. He trained a crew to mass-produce designs from his original stencils on panels for chests, cabinets, tables and dresser drawers. After their stencil work was done, he and my mother added individual accents and details by hand.

One spring day in 1959, when I was eight, my mother and father were on the back porch doing the finishing detail on wooden panels. "We're nearly done with the job for this company," Father said to her. "Nothing left but the hand-painting that only you and I can do."

"So, what about the crew?"

"We can't afford to keep them. I suppose we ought to let them go tomorrow. Will you do it?" he asked her, pleading. Although he could make himself look stern, he was extremely tenderhearted. Tasks like letting his crew go disturbed him greatly.

Mama groaned. "No, I can't."

"Okay. I'll do it, but I want you there," he said.

The next night my parents were playing bridge with friends. We three girls frolicked in the attic, raising a riot to attract attention. After several scoldings from Mother failed to quiet us, we heard a slow, heavy step on the stair. We were surprised to see Father, since he rarely raised his voice to us. His face looked drawn and tired, and he was very upset.

"I don't want to hear another peep out of you kids," he said angrily. He turned from the door, leaving three shocked little girls in his wake.

"What's wrong with Daddy?" my younger sister whispered.

"Shush," I hissed, thinking we must have done something terrible. When I pulled the sheet over my head, a tear trickled down my cheek. Daddy hadn't kissed us good-night.

The following morning I awoke to unfamiliar voices and muffled cries coming from downstairs. I heard my mother's footsteps climbing toward our room. She entered and sat on my older sister's bed. As we huddled next to her, tears rolled down Mama's cheeks. "Your father's gone," she said. "He had a heart attack during the night, and he died."

I felt as if someone had socked me in the stomach.

"Was it our fault?" my younger sister sobbed.

"No, honey."

"But, Mama," my older sister persisted, "we aggravated him a lot last night. He was real mad at us."

"He wasn't mad at you girls. He just wasn't feeling well."

Even though my mother said this, my father's angry face flashed before my eyes. I yearned to tell him how sad I was for making him angry, and I longed to hear him say in his soothing voice, "It's okay, dolly."

After his death, my mother seemed preoccupied all the time. She kept taking away mementos of my father. The mandolin disappeared, and the piano lid fell across the keys to gather dust. She took my father's chair from the supper table and put it in a closet.

My grandmother came to live with us while my mother struggled to continue the business. Budgets and meal plans appeared on the insides of kitchen cabinets as cruel reminders that money was tight. Our house was without song.

A few weeks later, I spied my mother sitting in the living room with a small flat box on her lap. Tears cascaded onto the cardboard cover like oversized raindrops. "What is it, Mama?"

She lifted her eyes in my direction with a distant look on her face. "It's something I bought for your father before he died."

"Don't you want to open it?"

"Not just yet," she said, rising and placing the box high on a bookshelf.

Occasionally I caught myself peering up at the mysterious box on the bookshelf, wondering what it was. But it remained there, untouched, and eventually I forgot about it.

Two years later on a warm summer afternoon, I was sprawled out on a chaise longue on the back porch, reading. Suddenly music exploded from our house. Great rich, echoing tones of Italian brought my father's face instantly before my eyes. I got up and went into the kitchen, where my grandmother was cooking. "Grandma, what's that music?" I asked.

She replied, "Something your mother bought for your father."

I knew then that the music had to have come from that mysterious box on the bookshelf. Running into the living room, I glanced up and saw that the box was missing!

I peeked into the dining room, where we kept our phonograph. Seated in a corner, lost in that soaring, wonderful sound, was my mother. She sat erect, staring out the window as if in a trance. I tiptoed over to the record player and picked up the record jacket. The round face of a small man with a paper-thin mustache and slicked-back black hair smiled at me. The record title read "Caruso's Greatest Hits."

Looking deep into Enrico Caruso's eyes as the music flooded my ears, I felt my father's presence. His music was filling the house once more. There was no escaping the pounding, trilling sounds of the Italian words. I tiptoed out, leaving my mother with her reveries.

Each day at dusk, Mother would sit in the dining room as Caruso's music washed over her, tears silently rolling down her cheeks. Several times I joined her. She'd smile at me, but then she'd disappear somewhere deep inside herself.

One father is more than a hundred schoolmasters.

GEORGE HERBERT

One day while the music played, my mother motioned for me to come sit next to her. She held my hand, and a smile warmed her face. "I was just thinking about the day before your father died," she said. "He was up to his old tricks."

"What do you mean?"

"He told me we needed to fire the crew, and we agreed to do it together. The next day at work, around four o'clock, he told me he had to take the car to the shop, and he disappeared. He left me at the factory with no choice but to fire the crew myself. The rat! I was going to give him a piece of my mind when we got home that night. But he sneaked up behind me with that sheepish grin and danced me around in a circle. The old trickster knew he'd pulled another fast one on me.

"After he'd had the heart attack, that night, I tried to keep his spirits up. I was teasing him in his hospital bed, saying, 'Don't you get sick and duck out on me with all this hard work facing us. You owe me one since you trapped me into firing the crew.' He patted my hand, smiled and asked me to get him some water. It was his way of tricking me again. He died while I was out of the room."

"Why did he do that?" I asked.

"Your father loved to make people happy; he never wanted to disappoint anyone. That was a real problem at times," she said ruefully. "I was so mad at him for dying. He died on a Friday, and on Monday morning I was at the factory finishing the job he and I were supposed to do together. I told myself I was mad at him because he'd left me with all that work. But I was mad because I missed him so much."

"I thought Daddy was mad at me," I said. "I thought our roughhousing upset his heart and he died. And I felt guilty."

"Joanie," she said, "don't feel guilty for another second. God sets the time. It was his time to go. Your daddy loved you girls more than anything—more than laughter, music, even his painting. And he left us all those gifts so we'd be strong enough to go on without him."

Throughout that summer my mother played those Caruso records again and again. While my friends twisted to Chubby Checker, I spent my afternoons humming tunes from "*Vesti la giubba*" and "*La donna è mobile.*" As I sat on the back porch and allowed the music to sink into my soul, I'd shut my eyes tight and see my father's dark, handsome face.

Finally one afternoon in late August, my mother lifted the record out of the player. She sighed, placed the record back in the jacket and slowly closed the phonograph. "That's enough," she said. "We're strong enough now." There were no traces of tears on her cheeks; her pale face was tranquil.

Shortly thereafter a man came to tune our piano. Mama retrieved the yellowed sheet music and began playing the familiar tunes. Sometimes all three of us girls gathered around her at the big brown piano. And we laughed and sang just the way he would have wanted us to.

KNOWING BRENDA

BY

JACQUELINE GUIDRY

$\mathcal{A}$cute infection of the spinal canal struck when they were six months old, killing my cousin Glenda and leaving her twin, Brenda, with a mangled body. I was born two months later, so I can only imagine the black hole of loss pulling at my family, their joy at the birth replaced by their grief at the death of one child and the seeming destruction of another.

Brenda could not walk or crawl; the only sounds she could make to attract attention were guttural cries. Her fingers dug into her palms, clenched even when the rest of her relaxed. Her stick limbs twisted back on each other.

But Brenda had eyes the blue of a sky after a hurricane. Her hair was pale yellow, soft as the down of a dandelion, thin as threads of silk. Her skin was nearly translucent, inviting touch with its smoothness, delicate as any newborn's cheek. She carried a distinctive fragrance, baby powder mixed with the smells of a body unmarked by the contamination of common life. When she smiled, those muscles being among the few she could control, her face lit with innocence. And if you wiggled a finger through her clenched ones, she held you tightly, silently promising to never let go.

My cousin Brenda lived at the center of our family. Her older sisters learned to tote her on their hips, and late afternoons they would troop across the pasture that separated our homes. Each visit, though ordinary and predictable, was occasion for an extravagant welcome. My mother and grandmother would beg Brenda for "sugar," a family euphemism for kisses. My brothers, faces dirt-streaked, dropped quick pecks on her cheek. She responded with a grin, magnanimous in her role as ruling heavenly body of our cosmos.

We girl cousins sat on front-porch rockers, Brenda balanced on a sister, the talk swirling around her. We spoke to her only occasionally, but she surely knew, and felt, how much she was a part of our afternoon chats.

Her presence invited the sharing of secrets. Some days we mused about the confessions she would've shared had she been able. When we spoke of her, she favored us with a smile. But it was the smile of a Mona Lisa, one that promised much and revealed nothing.

She could not speak, but was eloquent. When my uncle returned from work, he carried her from her living-room cot to his favorite recliner. He spoke of his day and hers, and she listened. She could not encourage him with questions or respond with her own thoughts, but her eyes never left his face. She listened with every atom of her being.

For months after he died, Brenda stared at her father's chair when the time of his expected return from work drew near. When he didn't appear, she sent forth low moans, her sorrow laid bare for all to hear.

Since Brenda could not use words, it was impossible to determine how much or how little she knew or understood. Two plus two equals four? Perhaps. That she lived on a planet called Earth spinning on its axis and circling in a set path around a burning star called the Sun?

Perhaps. That she was loved and treasured by parents and sisters, aunts and uncles and cousins? Absolutely.

Brenda taught us lessons that could pilot lives. To know Brenda was to know that the need to understand and be understood is deeper than the ability to speak—and that the limitations of birth or accident do not have to frame an existence.

Doctors said Brenda would never reach adolescence. Perhaps they could not imagine the power of love strong enough to propel a child through a dangerous universe. Brenda lived to her mid-thirties. And for each of those years, those of us who knew Brenda learned that we all ache for love and acceptance—and thrive when we receive them.

Whoever receives one such child in my
name receives me.

MATTHEW 18

MY BROTHER'S WAY

BY

IRA BERKOW

*C*oming back to New York from a trip to Minneapolis, I stopped in Chicago to visit my parents. One evening the phone rang. It was my younger brother, Steve. "Just a minute," I said after an uncomfortable pause. "I'll get Ma or Dad."

"Okay," he replied.

That was our entire conversation. We had hardly said much more than that to each other for the past few years. He had stopped speaking to me and never told me why. I had tried reaching out to him a few times but had always felt rebuffed.

Over the years Steve and I had a fluctuating relationship. A separation of five years in age makes a big difference when you're young. In my late twenties I had moved to New York to become a sportswriter for the Newspaper Enterprise Association, while Steve had become a teacher in a Chicago grade school.

My parents regularly urged us to reconcile. You only have one brother, they told each of us. You should be friends.

A few weeks later I was speaking to my parents on the phone and heard trouble in my mother's voice. Steve, she told me, was to begin chemotherapy.

"Chemotherapy?" I said, taken aback. "Why?"

Three years earlier Steve had been told that he had chronic lymphocytic leukemia, but the disease was nonaggressive; he would most likely live to 70. Somewhere along the line, however, his situation changed dramatically.

After hanging up, I sat by the telephone. Should I call Steve? The attachment to my brother, no matter how distant, was still there, still real. I felt it in my bones.

I was still stalling when my brother beat me to it. "I want to talk to you," he said after I answered the phone. "Don't you think it's about time we stopped this nonsense?"

"I've tried," I said. "You were the one who stopped talking to me."

"But you never asked me what was wrong," he replied. Then he told me that at an event two years earlier, I had neglected to introduce him to former White Sox pitcher Saul Rogovin, though I had introduced our father to Rogovin. I didn't remember the incident, and now I apologized.

The ice broken, we talked about day-to-day concerns. I asked how he was feeling, and he said the chemo was rough, "but if it's going to do good, then good."

"If there's ever anything—" I began.

"I know," he said. "I know that."

We talked about work. Steve taught eighth grade at Yates Elementary School in a kind of no-man's-land between black gangs to the west and Latino gangs to the east. Steve had drifted into teaching. For the first several years after college he had looked around for other things to do, but nothing else satisfied him or worked out. And then slowly, he grew more committed to his work with kids, until it took hold of his mind and heart.

He really cared about his students. He visited their homes, talked with their parents, made sure they had something to eat before school began, took them to places he loved that they otherwise might never visit, like the Chicago Botanic Garden.

I was proud of my brother. And I had told him so, although sometimes I'm not sure that I convinced him. I assumed that for Steve there were difficulties in being the less visible brother.

But even while growing up, Steve had to live in my narrow shadow, the way younger brothers often must. Not only was he younger; he was also short and very shy. I was less reserved, and I was also athletic. But a childhood case of measles had left Steve nearly blind in one eye, which made playing sports hard. His glasses were often falling off, getting fogged up, and breaking. I tried to show him how to throw a baseball, how to wind up and pitch, how to hit. Sometimes he'd listen, but other times he'd throw the bat down in frustration.

Once, he confided in me that he had considered going out for the high school baseball team. "But I wanted to live with the idea that I *could've* made the team," he said. "Maybe it was a way to save face if I hadn't made it."

One of his heroes was Paavo Nurmi, a Finnish track star of the 1920s. On the wall above his bed, Steve had taped Nurmi's photograph. He admired him, he once told me, because "he tried real hard. He was 75 to 80 years old, and he was still running. Still trying. Still determined."

I'm sure I kidded him about that old track star. Probably in reaction to my teasing, Steve would sometimes tell me to "get lost" if I asked him to help me out. Once, I was home on crutches after spraining my ankle in a basketball game, and I asked Steve to get me a hot dog from a place nearby. He refused. I had to pay his friend 25 cents to get me the frank.

About seven years later, when Steve was a freshman at Southern Illinois University, he called our parents to tell them he was homesick and wanted to leave. They asked me to call him. I talked for quite a while; I thought it was best for him to stay in school and told him why. I followed up with a letter.

A few days later I received a reply. "Dear Ira," he wrote. "Thank you for writing me. I really appreciate your advice because I realize quitting school could have started a chain of quitting. It's the most wonderful feeling when you have someone to turn to when you need help. Any time you want a hot dog, I'll run out to get it. Love, Steve."

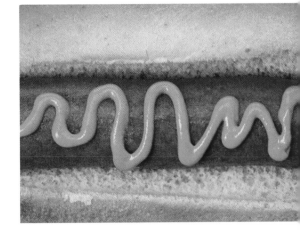

And now talking to Steve on that February night, I realized that there was in his voice a determination to patch things up between us again.

Steve was in and out of the hospital getting chemo over the next few months. I shuttled between New York and Chicago, and at the end of April I spent several days with him. "Look at this," Steve said, as he showed me a bunch of hair on his pillow. "It's all falling out. I told the doctor, I didn't say I wanted to look like Michael Jordan; I just said I wanted to play like him."

The following afternoon we talked about mortality. "I feel I've been blessed," Steve said, "But Ira, I don't want to go now. Judy and me—we have places we want to go and see. And I want to see Shayne graduate from high school. I—" He turned toward the window.

"I know," I said. "I know."

On my next visit to Chicago I saw Steve's internist. I wanted to hear from him what the prognosis was. "Your brother has virtually no immune system," he told me bluntly.

"Is this going to take a miracle?"

"Miracles happen."

After I left him, I went to see Steve. My parents, Steve's wife Judy and their daughter Shayne were there. When it was time for me to leave for the airport, I walked over to my brother and put my hand on his shoulder. "I love you, Steve," I said.

"I love you, Ira. C'mere." He grabbed my jacket, pulled me to him and kissed me on the check. I turned to my family, waved good-bye—and walked out. If I had tried to speak, I would have cried.

I just said it, I thought on the way to the airport. I said, "I love you." I had never told my brother that before. He had never told me, either. How strange. Why was it so hard?

I felt a sense of fulfillment, of deep satisfaction, in having finally expressed my feelings to my brother. Of course, I had Steve to thank for making the first move. In the end the younger brother had taken the role of the older brother.

I spoke with him by telephone a short while later. "The hospital rabbi came to see me," he said. "We spoke for about an hour, and I got a little emotional—I cried twice."

"You did?" I asked. "When?"

"Well, once when the rabbi held my hand."

"And the other time?"

"The other time was when I told the rabbi about you."

Four days later Steve developed critical pneumonia and was put on a respirator. I went to visit him in the ICU and spoke to him, though I had no idea whether he could hear me. His eyeglasses were on the table near him. Good, I thought. When he gets better, he'll have his glasses right there. He'd want that.

But there was no miracle. The end came on Tuesday, May 21. I held his hand, I told him again that I loved him, then I kissed him on the forehead and said good-bye.

When brothers agree, no fortress is so strong as their common life.

ANTISTHENES

At Steve's funeral the chapel was standing room only. Old and young, men and women, blacks and whites. It was wonderful. Steve's entire eighth-grade class had come. "More of the kids wanted to be here," a student told me, "but the principal said they couldn't have the whole school empty."

After the service Judy showed me letters from students, telling her how Steve had urged them to go on with their education and advised them on how to deal with problems in the streets and with their families. Wrote one student, "He wasn't just a teacher—he was my best friend. Every time I needed help, he would never let me down." Another student, on hearing of Steve's death, had taken down the flag in the classroom and folded it up. He presented it to Judy a week later.

None of us in the family had had any idea how my brother had so profoundly affected his students' lives. I'm not sure even he realized it.

I considered what makes a person important. There are the people in the spotlight whom we honor but who often go about their lives in selfish pursuits. Then there are the people like Steve, who make a hands-on difference but for whom no monuments are built, no streets named, no parades thrown.

I visited my brother's grave site a month after he was buried. There was a simple marker—a larger one would replace it in a few months—which read "S. Berkow." It was still so unbelievable I began to choke up.

A pot of flowers lay beside the grave, placed there by Judy and Shayne a day earlier. I had brought my own tribute to Steve—this good and blessed and brave man. From my pocket I took a photograph from a sports magazine and placed it on his grave. It was a picture of Paavo Nurmi, running like hell.

LOVE IS NOT ENOUGH

BY

MARGARET STERN MATTISSON

My husband Mike and I sit in the third row of the audience, waiting for our Katie's name to be called, waiting for Katie to graduate. Mike presses my hand and smiles. We are proud and grateful. There was a time when I could not have imagined Katie's graduation from college. I remember that time . . .

Dress rehearsal of *H.M.S. Pinafore* was well under way at our community church. As a member of the chorus, I stood in my stiff, shiny pink gown with nine other women—all housewives like me who had volunteered to do the show for "Fun and Funds." One of the church secretaries entered, signaled to get my attention and mouthed, "Telephone." I headed for her office, sure it would be Mike having to work late, or Joe, our eldest, calling from college, or Jimmy, held up at football practice, or Katie, our conscientious 16-year-old, wondering what to defrost for dinner.

"Hello," I said. There was no answer.

"*Hello,*" I repeated, and heard a faint, muffled, "Mother, come home." It was Katie. Something was wrong.

"What's the matter?" I cried.

"Come home . . . come, please," was the only answer. I hardly recognized her voice.

"I'm coming, Katie, but what *is* it? What's happened?"

"I've taken sleeping . . . sleeping . . . sleep . . ." I heard the phone crash to the floor. And no more.

For a brief, awful moment, I didn't move, paralyzed by fear. Then I began fumbling in my purse for the car keys. "Please," I managed to say to the secretary, "get an ambulance to my house. Get Katie to the hospital." And then I fled to my car.

I arrived at the hospital just after Katie's ambulance. They would not let me see her.

Shaking with fright, I called Mike's office. "Come to the hospital, Mike. Something's terribly wrong with Katie," I gasped. For the first time, I broke down in sobs.

The desk nurse took the phone from me and led me to a small waiting room from which I could watch Katie's door. I still had on my *Pinafore* costume. I didn't care.

As the minutes steamrolled by, reality began to hit me. Katie had taken sleeping pills. *Sleeping pills.* Deliberately. A word formed in my mind. I barred it. It formed again. I couldn't bare it. *Suicide.* Katie had attempted suicide! No. Not Katie. Never!

Katie was the most loved and wanted child in the world—the perfect child—our pride and joy. She had honey-colored curls and eyes as blue as the sky. Her teachers, from the day she entered nursery school, adored her, though at times we thought they praised her just a bit too much. In junior high school, when the other kids fell into the early-adolescent patterns that bewilder parents, Katie remained a joy. She

didn't giggle with the girls about sex, or go boy crazy; she didn't shoplift or smoke pot. She was elected a class officer every year, and three years in a row won the Outstanding Citizen Award.

Mike and I never pushed her to achieve; she just did. She got good marks, was usually on the honor roll, played the piano, wrote poetry and did her homework faithfully. How we loved her!

My reverie was broken by Mike's frantic arrival at the hospital. I rushed to him and we pressed each other's hands tight. Just then a doctor opened the door to Katie's room. We saw her still, sheet-covered figure on a table. Tubes led to and from her like wires on a switchboard. The doctor came over to Mike and me. They had pumped Katie's stomach, he said. She was still unconscious, but they thought she would be all right. One of us should stay with her. We nodded, knowing we would both stay.

"Who is your psychiatrist?" the doctor asked. Mike and I exchanged incredulous looks. "We don't have one," Mike said.

"I'll send the staff man then." His voice was matter-of-fact. "You'd better go into her room now. We may have trouble when she wakes up."

Katie lay on a narrow bed. Mike and I sat, he at the foot and I at the side. I took Katie's hand. It was cold, unresponsive. An hour passed. Two hours. An unspoken question thundered between us: *Why?*

Why, indeed? Katie was good. Katie was successful. Katie was loved. Katie got along with her friends and teachers, with her brothers and even—wonder of wonders—with her parents. So why?

There was no answer.

When time had lost all frame of reference, Katie began to groan. As the groaning increased, her body began to move erratically from side to side.

"Katie," I whispered. "Katie, it's Mother and Dad. We're here." Her groaning increased; her lips tried to form words; her body thrashed.

Wiping her forehead, I put my face to her cheek. "It's Mother and . . ." Before I could finish, Katie spat out a mouthful of epithets that sent me reeling, stunned, back into my seat. Katie had never sworn before.

Mike left to get the nurse. They returned at once, the nurse carrying some gray bands that looked like army belts. She proceeded to strap down Katie's ankles and wrists, working coolly, wordlessly. Katie heaved under the restraints, her face drawn tight, her back arching to pull free. As the nurse ran a damp cloth over Katie's cheeks, Katie snapped like an animal, biting the nurse on the wrist. And out came a new string of curses.

So the night passed. For short spells Katie rested. For longer ones she twisted, pulled, screamed and spat her hate. When an intern untied her arms to examine her, she swung a fist and blood-ied his nose. And she kicked the glasses off a new nurse who tried to change her bed sheets. Finally, around six A.M., she fell asleep.

When Katie woke up later that morning, she tried to speak, but her mouth was too dry. I held a glass of water to her lips. I untied the straps that held her. She smiled. Mike and I spun toward each other. We held back tears.

"Where am I?" Katie murmured.

"In the hospital, Katie," Mike answered.

Katie rubbed her wrists. "I dreamed . . . I thought I dreamed." She stopped, her face a frown of confusion. "I can't believe I . . . all those things . . . I sort of remember . . . I hated everything, everyone."

"Us, Katie? Mostly us?" Mike asked.

"No. Mostly me," she said, and closed her eyes.

A little later, Dr. Mathews, a staff psychiatrist, came in. He asked Mike and me to leave, then stayed with Katie for an hour. When he came out, he took us into a small office. "Katie is a very upset young woman," he said. "She doesn't think much of herself. That's why she took sleeping pills."

"But she's wonderful—always has been," I blurted out defensively. "She *must* know it."

Dr. Mathews kept calm. "She knew you thought so, and she tried to be, felt she *had* to be, what you thought she was. That's what she was telling us last night."

"Why that way?" I asked. "Why didn't she just tell it to us before? We always talked."

"She didn't want to disappoint you—didn't want anyone to think she wasn't as nice as they all thought she was. We all want to be loved, you know. She thought acting nice is what made people love her—even her parents. She doesn't think she is a person, so dying doesn't matter. That's my concern now."

"Then she might do it again?" Mike asked.

"Yes. That's why I want to put her in a psychiatric hospital for a while."

Mike and Dr. Mathews continued talking, but I did not hear them. My mind blacked out. I came back into the world—dizzy and unbelieving—to hear them decide on the hospital to which Katie would go. "You know, she's not the first. There'll be other young people there," Dr. Mathews said. He got up and walked around the desk to us. "She loves you, you know."

"And we love her," Mike said.

"I know."

"Then, why?" I pleaded.

"Love is not enough. You can't exist as the reflection of someone's love. You have to be your own person." There was a long silence. "She will be."

We returned to Katie's room. She was lying on her back, her head to one side, her hair falling across the pillow. Outside she looked peace-

The joys of parents are secret, and so are their griefs and fears.

FRANCIS BACON

ful—like the Katie we had thought we knew. Inside—where we had never seen—seethed resentment and self-loathing, bound up by the image of our love as painfully as her wrists had been bound during the night.

Katie spent five months in the hospital. She missed that year of school, and decided not to go back in the fall. Instead, she got a job in a local store. We said nothing; we were learning to understand.

By December, she felt she was ready. She returned to school as a junior and graduated a year and a half later. And that September she entered college.

Mike looks over at me and pats my hand. Katie's name has been called. As she walks to the platform, the speaker announces her achievements—a bachelor's degree *magna cum laude,* with election to Phi Beta Kappa. Katie finds us with her eyes on her way back to her seat. She smiles and gives a little shrug of her shoulders.

Afterward, everyone congratulates us. Mike and I smile, and say polite thank-yous. Only he and I and Katie know that underneath this ritual of manners lies the real "thank-you"—for something she has struggled for and won far above her graduation honors. For that struggle, she has, at last, her reward.

She has her self.

A FATHER, A SON
AND AN ANSWER

BY

BOB GREENE

*P*assing through the airport one morning, I caught one of those trains that take travelers from the terminal to their gates. Free, sterile and impersonal, the trains run back and forth all day long. Not many people consider them fun, but on this Saturday I heard laughter.

At the front of the first car—looking out the window at the track that lay ahead—were a man and his son. We had just stopped to let off passengers, and the doors were closing again. "Here we go! Hold on to me tight!" the father said. The boy, about five years old, made sounds of sheer delight.

I know we're supposed to avoid making racial distinctions these days, so I hope no one will mind if I mention that most people on the train were white, dressed for business trips or vacations—and that the father and son were black, dressed in clothes that were just about as inexpensive as you can buy.

"Look out there!" the father said to his son. "See that pilot? I bet he's walking to his plane." The son craned his neck to look.

As I got off, I remembered something I'd wanted to buy in the terminal. I was early for my flight, so I decided to go back.

I did—and just as I was about to reboard the train for my gate, I saw that the man and his son had returned too. I realized then that they hadn't been heading for a flight, but had just been riding the shuttle.

"You want to go home now?" the father asked.

"I want to ride some more!"

"More?" the father said, mock-exasperated but clearly pleased. "You're not tired?"

"This is fun!" his son said.

"All right," the father replied, and when a door opened we all got on.

There are parents who can afford to send their children to Europe or Disneyland, and the children turn out rotten. There are parents who live in million-dollar houses and give their children cars and swimming pools, yet something goes wrong. Rich and poor, black and white, so much goes wrong so often.

"Where are all these people going, Daddy?" the son asked.

"All over the world," came the reply. The other people in the airport were leaving for distant destinations or arriving at the ends of their journeys. The father and son, though, were just riding this shuttle together, making it exciting, sharing each other's company.

So many troubles in this country—crime, the murderous soullessness that seems to be taking over the lives of many young people, the lowering of educational standards, the increase in vile obscenities in public, the disappearance of simple civility. So many questions about what to do. Here was a father who cared about spending the day with his son and who had come up with this plan on a Saturday morning.

The answer is so simple: parents who care enough to spend time, and to pay attention and to try their best. It doesn't cost a cent, yet it is the most valuable thing in the world.

The train picked up speed, and the father pointed something out and the boy laughed again, and the answer is so simple.

"IF WE STAY HERE, WE'LL DIE"

BY
FRANKLIN R. JONES

The gray New Hampshire landscape writhed in a slow, snake-like dance as I stared through the rain-streaked kitchen window. All that November morning, a fine drizzle had been falling.

"It's a rotten day," I grumbled. My nine-year-old daughter, Carolyn, resting her chin against my shoulder, had just reminded me of my promise to take her to see the porcupine caves. "Look, Carolyn, I'd like to. It's just that you'd get soaked."

"Oh," she said softly.

There was a long silence and I should have dropped the whole thing. Instead, I said, "Well, I suppose we could—if you take a hot bath when we come back."

We left the house just before noon. Carolyn wore dungarees and two light sweaters under a wool shirt. I had on wool pants, the top to my insulated underwear and a cotton shirt. Carolyn had made some peanut-butter sandwiches, and I had a few chocolate bars in my pocket.

We drove to the Flintlock farm, left the car by the main road and followed the old tote road into the woods. Walking in the warm rain, we made our way south through the woods, crossed the thick alder swamp, and climbed the ridge to a big outcropping of rocks. On the far side we found the porky caves—low, horizontal crevices cutting deep into the ledge. We explored them, but no animals were home.

The caves were not large enough to serve as a shelter, so I suggested we build a little lean-to. Long-dead branches served as a framework, and we gathered hemlock boughs to thatch the roof. We scrunched our wet bodies into this regal mansion and dined on soggy sandwiches and sticky chocolate bars, conversing on the splendors of nature and the benefits of being a wild animal.

As we talked, it occurred to me that the temperature had changed, and I was suddenly very chilly. "Let's go," I said. "It's two o'clock, anyway."

We had moved only a hundred feet when I felt the cold bite at my cheeks and seep through my wet pants. Then we saw the first flakes of snow mingled with the rain. By the time we reached the swamp, the sky was a whirling mass of blinding white snow.

Even in good weather, it's difficult to cross the swamp unless you take a bearing on the opposite shore. I had always sighted on a tall pine that stuck up above the rest of the woods. But now, engulfed by snow, I could hardly make out bushes 20 feet ahead.

We crossed the swamp and headed through the woods, fighting the wind, trying to watch the way and keep the snow out of our faces at the same time. Then Carolyn stopped. "There's our house," she said, nodding her head toward the right.

"What house?"

"Our little house—right there."

"You mean our lean-to? No, that's just some old branches . . ."

She crossed the clearing, stopped and spun around. Her voice was calm, quite matter-of-fact. "It *is* our lean-to."

"Now, that was pretty bright," I said, trying to smile. "You know what happened? I was too busy fighting the snow to pay attention. We've walked in a circle."

Carolyn showed little interest in my theories. She was shivering. "I'm cold," she said.

"Okay—we'll just have to try again." We went back to the swamp, and again I led her to the far side. Carolyn stomped one foot and then the other. "My sweater's freezing," she said.

"Look, honey, you stand here a minute. I'll go along the edge here and find the big pine." I walked slowly, keeping her in sight. I kept talking so she would not be scared. Gosh, she was good. Not a complaint about my blundering.

There was no tree. I went back and tried the other direction. Everything looked strange. I didn't recognize a single landmark.

It was almost four. Hard to see my watch. Better move out, only this time I'd bear to the left more, toward the main road. We walked, and the snow whipped about us so thick that Carolyn couldn't look up. She took hold of my shirttail, and I pushed my way through windfalls and dragged her up snow-covered slopes.

Darkness was quick in coming, but the white of the snow made it possible to see the black branches that reached out for us. Carolyn fell and I pulled her up. A sob burst from her lips. "My feet hurt, Dad."

I ran my hand over her face and felt the crust of ice that encased her hair. "It's all right . . . you cry if you want to . . . I know you're cold."

"I . . . I'm all right."

We walked faster now. I literally dragged her along as she clung to my shirt. "I can't walk. I don't feel anything," she said.

It must have been the newspaper item I had read that first distorted my thinking. Just a little item I'd glanced at with only passing interest—about a man and his young son lost in the woods. It had been raining and the father tried to keep his son warm by holding him against his body. But the boy died of exposure before morning.

As we stumbled aimlessly through the woods, this news item flashed again and again across my dull mind. I wasn't kidding myself—I was in the same spot, maybe worse. The temperature had dropped fantastically since two o'clock. Both of us were encrusted in a thin layer of ice. My hands were numb with cold, and Carolyn was certainly colder.

I could see a dark mass against the sky. "Let's go to that ledge. I'll build a fire."

Suddenly, I stopped and stared through the trees. A gray piece of land, darker than the snow, had caught my eye. Even in the oncoming night I knew it was the swamp. I left Carolyn and stumbled toward it. I had to find out which side we were on. I walked a few yards, first in one direction and then the other. And then I knew—it wasn't the same swamp. This was the big swamp, deeper in the woods. But which side was I on?

I helped Carolyn to the rocks. I gathered leaves and twigs from under the crevices. Green pine needles were tenderly set on top of this tinder. I took out my lighter.

Until this moment, I was sure that my daughter had no doubts of my ability to handle the situation. Now she looked at my hands as I fumbled with the lighter. I struck violently at the wheel, again and again. There were sparks—feeble sparks that quickly died. A sob welled up from Carolyn's throat. She shook convulsively, then cried. I looked down at the little girl and realized that I was responsible for her life, and wasn't doing well at all.

Perhaps my insulated underwear would keep her warmer than her sweaters. I unbuttoned my shirt and told her to take off all her upper clothing. We threw the wet sweaters aside and she stood naked to the waist with snow falling on her quivering body.

To my amazement, the inside of my underwear was perfectly dry, even though we had been exposed to hours of rain and snow. Almost instantly Carolyn felt the warmth of the garment as I put it on her and fumbled to fasten the snaps. My own cotton shirt was less inviting as its icy wetness hugged against my flesh.

I needed a moment to think—to stand alone and try to unravel this terribleness I'd created. I climbed to the top of the ledge and stared into the gray, snow-filled sky. Never in my life had I faced a danger so real. Not for myself. I could keep walking all night to keep warm. But for my child. The newspaper article kept flashing like a neon sign. I had to do something.

Then I heard a sound. I turned my head quickly to pick out the direction. There it was again—the bark of a dog off to my right. It sounded a million miles away.

The silence that followed made me ill. Then I heard it again. For the first time during the storm my mind seemed to function clearly. It was only a chance—that dog might never let out another yap—but anything was worth trying now.

Carolyn lay huddled against the rocks and I knelt beside her. "Carolyn, you've got to listen. If we stay here, we'll die. We're going to walk out. There's a dog barking . . . we can follow the sound." She didn't answer.

I would have to make her walk. I'd never be able to carry her up and down the snow-covered ridges. "You've got to walk. Understand?"

She moved her head slowly from side to side, sobbing softly. "I didn't . . . hear a . . . dog."

"No mind, you can't hear him except on a ridge." I helped her to her feet. She held on to my shirttail, and we stumbled over the rough ground and half crawled up the slope of the next ridge. We couldn't hear anything but our own breathing. Then the dog barked again.

The regularity of that blessed dog's voice each time we struggled to the crest of a ridge became eerie. Always we stood for a few moments, then a couple of deep barks and silence.

But on the fifth hill there was no sound—only the gurgle of an underground brook somewhere. The soundless curtain of snow continued to fall. "We've got to try for another ridge," I said. "We just can't stand still too long."

I slid down the slope with Carolyn hanging on, and then we carefully moved ahead through the trees. We came into a clearing and I was about to cross over, when I realized we were standing in a road. A tote road! "We did it, honey, we did it!"

But I wasn't sure. Was it the right road—and which way should we go? I decided to turn left and we moved slowly, guided by the light strip of snow. We'd gone about 20 yards when I felt logs under my feet. I stomped my foot and knew by the sound that I was standing on a bridge.

We had walked over a bridge on the way in. I got down on all fours and ran my stiff fingers over the end of each log. Then I repeated the same thing on the other end.

"What are you doing, Dad?"

"Here it is, Carolyn—the nail! I remember a nail on the far end of this bridge. I caught my boot on it once. We're going the wrong way—*that's* the way out. We made it, Carolyn!"

We made it, all right, and found our car at the end of the old road. A dog up at the farm barked as I slammed the door. It was the same deep bark, bless his soul.

It is a wise father that knows his own child.

SHAKESPEARE

I was sure we'd been lost most of the night, but it was only six o'clock and supper was being set when we got home. We couldn't tell them—not just then. We went in and I helped Carolyn take off her wet things and she got into a hot tub. Then I carried her to the living room bundled in a blanket and had her drink some warm wine.

As I was lighting my pipe, she reached for my sleeve and pulled me close, and kissed my cheek. "Thanks, Daddy, for bringing me out."

Give a little love to a child, and you get a

great deal back.

JOHN RUSKIN

IN GOD'S HANDS

BY

ROBERT A. CALCAGNI

The telephone call came one Saturday in August. They were going to operate on Monday morning. The next afternoon I was 35,000 feet above the Atlantic Ocean, headed for the States, half-convinced my family would remember 1991 as the year my father died.

His chances were poor, the cardiologist had said, but surgery was the only way to bypass his clogged arteries and repair the defective valves in his exhausted heart.

"What should I do, Bob?" My father had asked a few weeks before, when my work in Europe last allowed me to visit. It was a question I dreaded, because I knew he would do whatever I advised. Then if he died on the operating table, or turned down the surgery and lived just a few more miserable months, I would be left with the guilt.

I closed my eyes, listening for the voice of God, and said, "Let's go for it, Dad."

Now, heading home again, staring into the endless blue sky, I saw my father as I often do in the landscape of my mind: a nine-year-old immigrant at Ellis Island, clutching his mother's hand and looking up at the stranger who is *his* father. A decade before, my grandfather had left an Italian mountain village to seek his fortune in the New World; it had taken all those years to save enough to send for his wife and the son he had never seen.

He took them to Youngstown, Ohio, a booming steel town. It was hard for a nine-year-old boy. Uprooted, teased for his faltering English, my father grew up cautious about expressing emotions that might be laughed at. Even after he married and had children of his own, he found it hard to put into words what he felt. But he worked hard and in the toughest times we three kids always had warm beds, clean clothes, good food and a quiet place to study. That's how he showed he loved us.

My father rarely saw his own family, but he was endlessly astonished by my mother's. The Leones, seven brothers and sisters and their spouses, all lived within a few blocks and were one another's best friends. They barely made a distinction between siblings and cousins, and we kids, some two dozen of us, were raised as one inseparable clan. My dad was pulled into this open-hearted circle of kin, who embraced him unconditionally.

Still, not until he was confronted by his own mortality did he find it within him to respond. In his fifties he was stricken with diabetes. Later, he almost died in an auto accident, and he suffered a stroke. Then his heart began to fail.

Always, his wife and children were there, love and concern plain in their eyes. Finally, one day he took my mother's hand and said the magic words at last. "I love you," he told her. Looking around at all the in-laws crowded into his sickroom, he added: "I love you all."

I arrived at the Cleveland Clinic in time for a short visit the night before my father's surgery. He was calm. "Either way, the good Lord will look after me," he said.

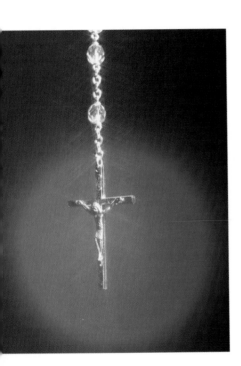

I believed that too. But he had come so late in life to accepting his family's love that I wanted desperately for us all to have a few more years together.

Early the next morning, I was glad to see my aunts, nieces, nephews and cousins arriving at the hospital. Loyal as ever, the Leones had driven the 80 miles to Cleveland—on an ordinary workday—to sit through the long operation with my mother, my wife, my brother, my sister and me.

I found a seat in the cramped waiting room next to my cousin Ray. Actually, he was more like an older brother. My very first memory is of the day the mill whistles blew, signaling the end of World War II; my second is of Ray swinging off a train in his khaki uniform.

There was family talk that something had happened to Ray in Italy during the war, but he never mentioned it. Once, when I tried to get him to tell, he grabbed a football and sent me running out for a pass.

Ray's presence in the hospital meant a lot to me for another reason. All the Leones were secure in their faith, but Ray's quiet, unshakeable conviction that God's hand is on each of us had helped us all through many a crisis. It was a family joke that he needed a new rosary regularly because "he works the beads so hard." The first thing he did when I sat next to him was to show me the new rosary his son had given him for Christmas.

Then suddenly it was afternoon, six hours after the operation had begun, and a doctor sought us out. They had not been able to get Dad off the life-support systems, and the surgeons were concerned.

No one missed the message: get ready for the worst. My mother began to cry.

"Wait a minute," I said instinctively. "It's not over yet." I turned to Ray and asked, "Let's say a rosary for Dad. Will you lead us?"

When he pulled the new rosary from its pouch, a little white tag fluttered to the ground, and I automatically picked it up and stuck it into my pocket while following his intonations: "Our Father, who art in heaven . . ."

Afterward, seeing that my mother had collected herself, I walked out for a moment's solitude. I found myself at the door to the operating rooms, as close to my father as I could get—while he was still alive.

Then Ray was there. He said a strange thing: "I want to tell you what happened in the war, okay?"

And he took me back nearly half a century, to a day in January 1944.

The U.S. Fifth Army, slogging north toward Rome, has been stopped dead at the Gustav Line, a German stronghold in the hills above Cassino. There, using the high ground around a sixth-century monastery as an observation post, enemy artillerymen pour shellfire on the beleaguered American troops. Then comes the order to advance. Pfc. Ray Leone, a Youngstown high-school student not long before, is squeezing his rosary and praying with all his might. One behind the other, the men of B Company move down the trail toward the Rapido River.

The foggy winter night is rent by the terrifying shriek of rockets and .88-mm shells. In the brief silences that follow, Ray can hear the anguished cries of the dying. With the piercing whine of each incoming shell, the men dive into every muddy fold and crevice. Then those who can advance a few more yards.

The company regroups. But German gunners pinpoint its position and zero in. *Help us, Lord,* Ray Leone prays. *There is nothing now, just you.* His face is pressed into the mud, but faith is his refuge.

A shell whistles past. *Oh dear God, is this it?* It hits five yards away, splashing everyone with mud—but there is no explosion. It's a dud!

"That one must've been made in Czechoslovakia!" someone yells, and men laugh, half-hysterical with relief.

Another dud splatters down. And another. "Made in Czechoslovakia!" Ray hears himself cry out.

Of course he doesn't know whether this is actually so. There has been barracks-talk of sabotage in the armaments factories of Nazi-occupied Europe, but that is just rumor. What matters is that God is answering his prayer. He has offered a shred of hope to cling to, and Ray lifts his head to spread the word: "Made in Czechoslovakia!"

With every shell that fails to explode, someone else takes up the cry. They envision secret bands of laborers somewhere in a defiant land, risking their necks to save the lives of unknown allies. "Made in Czechoslovakia" becomes an anthem, an answered prayer.

Battered B Company is eventually withdrawn across the Rapido. It will take four months and thousands of casualties before the Allies capture Monte Cassino; many who were there will never be able to speak of it.

Standing outside the operating rooms, Ray told me why. "There was a certain sense of guilt that I survived. I lived while better men died. They have been dead all these years, and I have been raising a family." He took a deep breath. "But now I have a reason to tell the story. Do you understand?"

I understood perfectly. There are things ruling our lives that do not conform to rules of reason. There is no evidence the Czechoslovakians or anyone else sabotaged German artillery shells. What was it, then, that

It is by believing in roses

that one brings them

to bloom.

FRENCH PROVERB

saved the remnant of B Company? Some people would call it luck. Wiser ones call it faith.

I was fingering the white tag in my pocket, about to show it to Ray, when I heard my name on the hospital intercom. For a split second I thought, *Dad's gone.* Then I knew better.

When Ray and I got back to the waiting room, everyone was smiling, and there were tears of joy on my mother's face. "Your father came through," the doctor told me. "Of course the next few days are critical, but . . ."

"He's going to be okay," I said flatly. "You'll see."

When Ray pulled out his rosary to say a prayer of thanks, I produced the white tag and said, "This fell out of the rosary pouch. Ever seen it before?"

"No," he said, looking at it, and our eyes filled with tears. Printed on the tag were three words: "Made in Czechoslovakia."

THE MOST ELUSIVE LOVE OF ALL

BY

SUE MONK KIDD

"*Ma*-a-a-ma! Come look!" Ten-year-old Ann was shouting at the back door.

Now what? I huddled in my favorite chair, enjoying a small oasis of quiet in what had been a frustrating day with my two children.

It was a week since school had ended, and suddenly the kids were home behaving like wild ponies let out of a corral. They jumped on the beds, chased the dog through the house, spilled soft drinks, grumbled about who got the TV remote, and whined that there was nothing to do—the perennial woes of summer vacation.

That morning, while watering my marigolds, they had drenched each other with the garden hose. Soggy tennis shoes, dripping clothes—it was too much. "Go to your rooms!" I yelled.

And that's how it had been all week. My face had taken on a certain grimace. Several times a day I stood the children before me and lectured them about their behavior, but nothing got through.

"Mama, come see!" Once again Ann's voice cut into the quiet. She glided to a halt beside my chair, breathless. "There's a chipmunk outside."

A chipmunk? "I'm reading," I explained.

"But Mama—"

"Not now." I tried to think of something to occupy her. Then I remembered. "Why don't you do your Sunday-school project?" She had come home last week with an assignment to make a booklet illustrating four ways to love someone: a teacher, parent, neighbor, friend—anyone she wanted.

"All right," she said, but her voice was so quiet I barely heard her.

In the late afternoon I peered into Ann's room. She had just finished her project. "Can I see?" I asked.

She twirled a lock of brown hair around her finger. "Come on," I prodded. Finally she relented, dropping the booklet into my hands.

"Four Ways to Love a Child" by Ann Kidd. I read the title twice. At once I saw: the booklet was meant for me. I started to tell her the idea was for her to show ways *she* could love someone, not ways *I* could love someone. But I kept quiet. Was she feeling so in need of love? I turned to page one.

"Go see chipmunks and stuff like that with your kids," it said. Beneath was a picture of a smiling mom and a little girl peeking around a tree at a chipmunk. I gazed at it, aware for the first time since vacation began that I'd treated the children more as interruptions than family members whose lives I wanted to share and enjoy. I looked up for Ann, but she had slipped from the room. I turned to page two.

"When kids mess up, give them some hugs." I smiled at her sketch of a mother and child reaching to embrace each other. Hugs had been rare this week, especially when the kids "messed up." I recalled the angry banishment to their rooms earlier in the day. Maybe the moments they messed up were the very times I should embrace them with the assurance that they were loved.

"Give kids a chance to talk" was scrawled on page three. I looked over the crayon drawing, thinking of all the lectures I'd delivered and of my tendency to run on about some grievance while the children stood there unable to squeeze in a single word. And I asked myself, shouldn't my children have the right to invoke silence from their parents long enough to get their own thoughts and feelings across? There was one more page.

"Laugh a lot," it said. I wondered if Ann was referring to the water follies she and her brother had had with the hose. Could laughter have shifted things into perspective and helped me see that it was, after all, only water?

I closed her booklet. Yes, the children had been difficult. But so had I—hoarding time without sharing it, disciplining without loving, lecturing without listening, even forgetting my sense of humor. In that moment, I knew that the love I showed in the small, nitty-gritty moments of whines and water fights, grumbles and interruptions, may be the most elusive love of all—and the most important. Ann sauntered back into the room and stared at the booklet still in my hand. I gave her a hug and a wink.

The next day I was puttering in the kitchen when through the window I spotted Ann's chipmunk. I dashed for her room, where she'd been dipping a brush into red tempura paint. "Come quick!" I cried. "The chipmunk's back."

She whirled around so fast that she tipped over the paint. As it ran across her desk, she reached for the jar and dragged her sleeve through the red puddle. For a split second I was about to give in to one of those frustrated outbursts that come with raising children. But just in time I remembered Ann's "Four Ways to Love a Child," and I laughed instead. It was, after all, only paint—and outside there beckoned a fleeting moment for us to capture and tuck away in a little girl's heart.

The best inheritance a parent can give his

children is a few minutes of his time each day.

O. A. BATTISTA

THE SUMMER OF
AUNT LIZ NOAH

BY

PEG BRACKEN

On a recent summer afternoon, looking out my kitchen window, I suddenly experienced an unexpected moment of mourning for all things brave and beautiful and funny that aren't around anymore, and especially for my Aunt Liz Noah.

Being Grandpa's younger sister, she was therefore my great-aunt, who'd painted pictures and illustrated books in New York's Greenwich Village, a cheerful spinster till age 35. But when she met John Noah, a splendid-looking actor, it was a swift, glorious, high-hearted romance. They honeymooned in Italy and resettled in the Village, where she presently produced a beautiful baby daughter who wasn't quite three when the tragedy happened: both baby and husband died together in a theater fire.

It nearly killed Liz Noah, who was still in the hospital with a breakdown when both parents began their deaths back in Kansas. Suddenly regaining her equilibrium, she packed her grief, bags and a trunkful of big-city hats to go back home and cope. (And coincidentally be there for me to visit and laugh with on our family vacations, for despite everything, she is the person I've laughed with most, more than with anyone.)

After they died, she stayed to construct—gradually—a workable life: reading, painting, teaching kids to paint, and riding Grandpa's amiable chestnut mare, old Kiwani Girl. To me, everything about Liz Noah was perfectly splendid: her strong aquiline nose and deep-set somber eyes, her leanness, her mane of silver-streaked dark hair, and her customary faded old riding pants and shirt.

Between her house and Grandpa's were eight well-populated blocks. You passed the Caramel Lady's house, 50 cents a pound, 60 cents with nuts. And the man-who'd-been-in-jail's house, which you walked past fast. And faster still past The Elms, the nursing home where old people in bathrobes shuffled around the yard on warm days. (I'd once asked Grandma if she'd end up there, and she'd said No, you only went there if you had neither chick nor child. It didn't occur to either of us, I'm sure, that Aunt Liz Noah had neither chick nor child.) And finally to Liz Noah's house, its blue front door opening into a quite different world.

In an ecru era, her bright-white walls were alive with paintings, lithographs, sketches, and the kitchen was her studio. It was all exactly right, from the rip-roaring Kandinsky behind the stove to the wine-skin hanging over the sill and the clay flowerpot in the bathroom full of lovely-smelling sandalwood soaps.

And everywhere were books. Which I read. I remember it was at Liz Noah's that I first encountered Anderson and Cather, Frost and Dickinson, Yeats and Henry James. (I've heard that lonely people underline a great deal, and it was true of Liz Noah. I remember one marked passage in particular about a voyage of Columbus's, an endless time of violent storms alternating with doldrums, when day after weary day the log's sole entry was a bleak: *This day we sailed on.*)

Then there were Liz Noah's hats, the trunkful she'd brought back from New York. She let me model them sometimes, and I'd look like a mushroom, for they were big, marvelous hats designed for a tall woman. I remember a lovely sea-green chiffon concoction, and a glorious red velvet, all tilt and feathers.

And we'd talk, swinging idly in the glider on the shady porch, and make rhymes, and she'd do funny spidery sketches for our growing collection of addled adages: *It's a wise child who spills his own milk. A rolling stone seldom bites.* (And if you think it impossible to depict a rolling stone in the

very act of not biting, you just haven't seen Liz Noah's work.) And she'd talk about the family. I remember asking her once what heredity meant.

"Well—" and here she dropped one eyelid smooth as a rolled-down window shade while the other eye stayed stark-staring open, a remarkably droll wink she had. "It's like this," she explained. "If your grandma didn't have any children and your mother didn't either, then you probably inherit a tendency not to have any children yourself. That's heredity." Which made everything crystal-clear momentarily till it clouded up again.

And often we'd stroll down the drowsing summer street to the hotel soda fountain for an Osage Orange Soda, a luscious medley of rich vanilla ice cream, yellow as a four-egg custard, and fresh orange juice and lots of fizz.

Oh, we had good times, Aunt Liz Noah and I, and I know now that someone to laugh and wonder and speculate with is rare and to be valued. And I valued Aunt Liz Noah, though not enough. Or so I think now.

The trouble is that growing up is a full-time job. So often—busy with it—you shelve the elderly relatives you formerly found fascinating. Or think about them only when you're there, so they come alive only when you show up, the way the refrigerator light goes on when you open the door.

After McKinleyville High, Ganister moved to a far meadow of my mind. Busy growing up, I didn't realize that growing old takes time and attention too.

Two springs later, Mama wrote me that one afternoon a neighbor noticed milk curdling on the Noah back porch. So she pounded on the locked door, then forced open a locked window and found Liz Noah lying on the floor, in pajamas.

"What are you doing?" asked Mrs. Ostigsen.

"I like it down here," Aunt Liz Noah answered, with asperity. "I'm going to grow potatoes under the bed."

"She could've too," said Mrs. O. with relish, to anyone who'd listen. So Aunt Liz Noah went to the hospital with a broken hip, though it mended fast and she was soon back home.

Increasingly, though, she couldn't or wouldn't cope; wouldn't dust, swab out the sink, put the butter away. Finally after three months' virtual starvation on tea and toast, she developed an all-over skin rash the doctor called pellagra. He then wrote Mama. But Mama couldn't persuade Liz Noah to come home with her, and the only solution was The Elms.

She'd been there a year when I saw her again. My husband and I were heading west in a secondhand car, and I asked him to disappear, briefly. I didn't want Mike to meet the Liz Noah I'd probably find here in this shabby, brown-linoleumed place with the ubiquitous handrailings and wheelchairs and bleak smells.

She was sitting by a window, wearing a crisp blue-and-pink house-dress—Liz Noah, in a housedress! I hugged her, feeling her narrow, delicate bones, fragile as matchsticks through the gingham, and I wanted to weep. She was lost in that atrocious dress. And her hair was a soiled-looking yellow-gray, cut in an institutional bob.

"I'm so glad to see you!" I said. Truth, but a lie too.

"It can't be much of a treat," she said, sounding like herself. But she was looking past me. "Where is—who is—" She stopped, frowning. "My words are all thumbs," she said, and tapped her wedding ring impatiently. She remembered my recent marriage but not my new name.

I told her, and felt clumsy saying I wanted Mike to meet her. Then why hadn't I brought him? But she dismissed that.

"I'm not dressed for it," she said. "How do you like this little number? Chanel, I think."

"It's awful," I said sincerely. "You're not really ready for old ladyhood yet." And I wondered then if anybody is; and now that I'm considerably closer to it myself, I still wonder. Because people assume you've turned into a nice old prudent somebody inside to match your white-hair-and-wrinkles costume, but ten to one you haven't. You don't *feel* different—everyone knows that. I understood Liz Noah when she lifted a scanty lock and said scornfully, "This isn't me. I've got thick, dark hair."

"I know," I said, and knew she valued my knowing.

But presently we were discussing important matters, the way we'd always done. Like, What rhymes with Schenectady? What color is Nevertheless? Why aren't old ladies supposed to cuss, just when there's a lot more to cuss about?

"Yes, and furthermore," she said, "do you know you're actually *tested* to see if you've brains enough left to weave those ugly potholders? They ask you, Who's President? Where's straight up? What day's today?" She stopped.

"What day is today?" she asked slowly.

We just looked at each other. The tiny, busy ticking of a bedside clock was loud in the room.

It was growing late. Aunt Liz Noah walked me out to the glassed-in porch, humid with limp green things dangling from pots. There I left her, prisoner of her years as I, in another way, was prisoner of mine, my young husband waiting for me down the block. And I prayed then, *Get her out of there*, though I knew there was only one way she'd ever leave. But I didn't care; it was no place for Liz Noah, no place at all.

And so we left Ganister behind us, Mike and I, wanting to cover some distance before nightfall. The low winter sun was bothering our eyes, especially mine, because I was crying. And thinking how awkward and messy crying is—eyes flooding, nose filling. In the long evolutionary climb, why couldn't people have evolved something neater?

And then I remembered, Liz Noah and I had once pondered the very same thing—wondered why not something tidier? I'd suggested, couldn't your knees turn green for a while, or maybe your elbows itch? Or—her idea—your earlobes grow gently longer till they finally tickled your collarbone and made you laugh? But crying, who needed it? Drizzle and drip, cough and blow—

And so I mourned, in concentrated fashion, for all lovable, warm, bright people who must grow old and die, especially my Aunt Liz Noah. I cried nearly all the way to Salina, where I had to stop crying to eat dinner. And at the old Victorian hotel there were down pillows and a nice old calico quilt on the nice old four-poster bed and my husband comforted me.

It was about three months later that my mother phoned me in Oregon from McKinleyville. Aunt Liz Noah had run away. Just like that. Or, anyway, walked out. One April day toward sundown, she'd packed an overnight bag, put on her old riding pants, shirt, and one of her three remaining fine old hats, and walked all the way down Main Street to move into the Grand Osage Hotel.

Kindly, the desk clerk accepted her registration, and wisely he called my mother, who drove over the next day. The sole drawback she could find, finally, was that no one had thought of it sooner.

Aunt Liz Noah was happier now; even sketching a little and sometimes holding court in the lobby, sitting tall. Financially it made sense too. Even with coffee-shop room service and the occasional attentions of a practical nurse, it cost less than The Elms. And what happened was that about a year later she went to bed complaining mildly of a strawberry-shortcake stomachache. It was a heart attack, though, and the next morning she was dead.

Camus wrote, somewhere, "In the midst of winter I finally learned that there was in me an invincible summer." I think of that lovely line now, whenever I think of my Aunt Liz Noah on her own personal independence day, that greening April afternoon. There she goes, the tall, frail stork of a lady, hair wispy under the gallant hat, walking purposefully down Main Street. I never heard which hat it was, but I always see her in the red velvet.

A child is not a vase to be filled,

but a fire to be lit.

RABELAIS

WITH A LITTLE LUCK

BY

PENNY PORTER

"Daddy! Look what I found!" Jaymee ran to Bill, cupping a hidden treasure. "What is it, honey?" Bill looked down at our youngest daughter and mopped his forehead. The late-summer heat was oppressive. Mother Nature wasn't being kind to southeastern Arizona. Drought had withered our pastures. Bill was running the pumps 24 hours a day to irrigate the crops. He had calves to vaccinate and hay to bale. This wasn't his day. Lately no day was.

Cautiously, Jaymee unfolded her hands. Cradled there was a tiny hours-old jackrabbit.

"Can I keep him, Daddy?"

Jaymee, then eight, had wanted a pet rabbit for years, but Bill was a rancher. He already had a filly picked out for her. He hadn't bargained on her liking rabbits more than heifers and horses.

"It'll die," he said. "Babies need a mama."

"Can't I try? Please!" Jaymee begged. "You always say, 'With a little luck, anything's possible.'"

Bill sighed. He couldn't stand more problems now. The doctor had told him to slow down and learn to relax a little.

Jaymee turned to me. Tears threatened. "Let's take him in the house," I said.

Cally, our calico cat, was nestled near the wood stove with her seven new kittens. *Was it possible to trick Mother Nature?* I wondered.

Jaymee and I fed Cally until she was stuffed. When her eyes closed, and purring began, Jaymee pushed the jackrabbit's searching mouth against the untapped nipple. The tiny creature clung like peanut butter to a spoon. For three days, he grew fatter, and Cally seemed to treat him like one of her own.

"See, Daddy, it's true—with a little luck, anything's possible!"

But on the fourth day, Cally looked at this "kitten" through slit eyes, and then a wail of anger filled the kitchen. Her jaws opened, and she pounced. Bill leaped up and grabbed Cally by the tail, and the inter-loper tumbled from her claws.

Bill scooped up the trembling creature and gave it to Jaymee. "Better try bottle-feeding him," he said.

Miraculously, the jackrabbit lived. Soon he was eating cereal—and growing and growing. Finally we set him free, happy knowing he had another chance at life.

Jaymee, petless again, resumed her campaign. "Please, Daddy, can't I have just one rabbit, a tame one this time?"

Bill looked at me for help. "What good is a rabbit?" he asked.

Jaymee's eyes grew round. "They bring luck!"

I knew it would take more than that to sway Bill Porter.

"Oh, please, Daddy? I'd join 4-H and show it like you do with the cattle and horses." She came closer, her brown eyes tugging at his heart. Suddenly her arms were around his neck, and in one quick movement she slipped a bag of jellybeans into his pocket. Jaymee knew jellybeans helped more than anything. And they helped now.

That weekend, we drove to Albuquerque, where Bill bought *three* New Zealand Reds—all females.

"Why three?" I asked quietly.

"A little extra luck," he whispered, glancing in the rearview mirror at the happy girl in the back seat.

"Their names are Twinkletoes, Marshmallow and Alice," Jaymee called, holding the bunnies up one at a time for her father to see. "And Daddy, they'll bring you lots of good luck. I promise!"

Three months later, Twinkletoes gave birth to six babies. Then Marshmallow produced eight. We were stunned.

"How did they get pregnant, Mama?" Jaymee asked. "They haven't been near a buck. And why didn't Alice get pregnant too?"

"The rabbit dealer made a mistake," I offered.

"He *lied* is what he did," Bill said. "Seventeen rabbits!"

"That means lots of luck!" Jaymee announced, trying to soften the blow.

Bill renamed "Alice" Abraham, which in Hebrew means "Father of the many," and secured him behind dividers on the east wall of the hutch.

Then our 12-year-old nephew, George, visited from Milwaukee. George hated cows and horses. But he *loved* Abraham. Two weeks after he went home, Twinkletoes produce a litter of nine, and Marshmallow, 11. Once more Bill was exasperated. "All right," he said, "how'd it happen this time?"

"It was George," said Jaymee. "He loves watching them 'do it.'" She showed Bill her journal, with its neatly recorded transactions. Under "Item," the name George appeared. Under "Charge," 25 cents. Every day George had begged Jaymee to put Abraham in with Twinkletoes or Marshmallow. So she charged him 25 cents a half-hour! At the bottom of a long column was "Grand Total," $4.75!

Jaymee now had 37 rabbits. Bill put more dividers in the hutch. "We'll soon be ordering rabbit feed by the truckload!" he grumbled.

I pointed out that, with the rabbits' arrival, his luck was changing for the better. Cattle prices were up. We'd had the best alfalfa season ever, and rain came.

"It has nothing to do with the rabbits," he said.

Twinkletoes became Jaymee's favorite. She came when called, and she even hopped on a collar and leash.

Then Twinkletoes got pregnant, and this time no one asked how. What difference did it make? Cattle prices were staying up. As even Bill recognized, all was well.

But when it was time to give birth, Twinkletoes got sick and was unable to line her nest. She lay on the floor of the hutch gasping, each breath, we thought, her last. Eight babies arrived soon after nightfall: wet, cold and barely alive.

"They're going to die, Daddy. What can we do?"

We lined a pizza pan with foil and wet paper towels, and laid the seemingly lifeless kits in a circle. Covering them with another wet towel, we popped them into the oven set at the lowest possible heat. We watched through the glass window as, one by one, the tiny lumps started to jerk and wiggle.

Jaymee beamed. "Just our luck," Bill said with a grin. Then he hugged her close.

Back in the hutch, Twinkletoes had made a remarkable recovery. By the next morning, eight warm bunnies were cuddled at the bottom of her nest. Bill, I could tell, was as proud as Jaymee that all had lived.

Eventually the day came when a buyer offered to purchase Jaymee's rabbits. We agreed to sell them, except for Twinkletoes.

Was it mere coincidence that Bill's luck suddenly soured? Cattle prices fell. Rains damaged the alfalfa. An irrigation well caved in.

Yet this time, Bill seemed different, more patient and relaxed. I wanted to believe it had something to do with a little girl and her rabbits. Perhaps not. But there could be no question that they had distracted him lately from his worries—and maybe reminded him that, above all, family is more important than horses and heifers.

Anyway, he had stopped complaining that the newspaper was late and began commenting on sunrises at breakfast. He found time to watch our daughter Becky's high-school volleyball team. He visited and telephoned our three grown children more often now. Things that had gone wrong began to right themselves again.

The family is the association established by nature for the supply of man's everyday wants.

ARISTOTLE

One afternoon, Bill returned from Tucson, where he'd gone to buy a fuel pump for the tractor. When Jaymee and I went to meet him, Twinkletoes hopped happily beside us.

As Bill climbed out of the truck, a worried Jaymee asked, "Daddy, do you think Twinkletoes is too old to have babies?" We had bred her twice, with no luck.

Pulling a box from the truck, Bill paused and smiled at Twinkletoes. "No, sweetheart," he said. "Mother Nature has just given her a chance to enjoy other things."

"Like taking a walk on a leash?"

"Well, sure—but more than that." Putting the box down, Bill leaned over and stroked the rabbit. "It's more like the happiness of knowing she's loved." He paused. "And knowing there's a big world out there that, with a little luck, she'll have time to enjoy."

Bill turned and opened the box. Suddenly his face darkened. "Damn!" he said. "They gave me the wrong pump. Now I'll have to drive one hundred miles back to Tucson tomorrow!"

"Can we go?" Jaymee asked. "It'll be Saturday, and we could have lunch. Just the three of us."

222

Bill's expression softened. "You know," he said, "there's a new Mexican restaurant in Tucson. After we pick up the pump, let's go there. Should be fun."

When Bill went to wash up, he was smiling. I noticed something else too: before all the chores and problems began to get him down, he had always gone about humming to himself. Now that a little girl and her rabbits had brought a bit of luck back into his life, Bill Porter was humming again.

ALL I EVER WANTED

BY

SUSAN E. JAMES

*W*hy, I pleaded with my mother, did I have to share a room with Linda? I was 12 at the time, and in my mind, at least, my seven-year-old sister was still a child. She went to bed earlier than I did, and the light was turned off at *her* bedtime. I had to resort to a flashlight under the covers if I wanted to read the latest Nancy Drew mystery.

Secretly, I meditated on the bliss of being an only child with a room all my own. And during that summer, my father seemed to be meditating along the same lines. He was going to night school and wanted a room to study in quietly, apart from his noisy family. So he decided to build one.

For my father, adding a room to the house was not a matter of calling in a contractor or an architect—it meant getting out hammer and saw, buying some nails, plaster and lumber, and getting to work.

We children were fascinated with the construction process. My baby brother toddled about the back yard with cries of "hammoah, hammoah" as he dragged behind him a hammer bigger than he was. When the framework went up on the concrete foundation, the room became a forest where we played Robin Hood. When the tar paper went

on, it became an Old West saloon where Wyatt Earp and the Clantons stared at one another down the barrels of six-shooters from Woolworth's. When the wiring went in, the metal slugs punched from the outlet boxes were gold nuggets that we miners prospected for in the mountains.

All through the summer the room rose like a miniature magic castle. Daddy built a bookcase into one wall for his schoolbooks, a large closet, and windows facing out in three directions. How I envied him the luxury of a room of his own.

As summer became autumn, work on the room slowed. Around Thanksgiving, there were sudden, freak snow flurries. Southern California is not known for such weather, and in my 12-year-old memory it had never snowed before. Through the windows of the partly completed room, I watched snow drift from the sky, catch on a net of spider webs strung between the branches of the maple tree, and then spin off toward the ground.

There was something magical about that moment. The room was cold because the heat had not been hooked up yet, and the floor was still bare plywood. But to me the room was the cave of the Mountain King. It was Snow White's castle with snowflakes drifting past the windows. I perched on an old stepladder—the only furniture in the room—and watched the back yard change into a world I had never before seen.

By Christmas, the room was finished—pale-blue walls, blue curtains shot with gold thread, floor laid, heat and electricity turned on.

On the last day before Christmas vacation, I came home from school and found the bedroom I shared with my sister completely rearranged.

"Okay, Linda!" I shouted. "What did you do with my books?"

Linda smiled her smug I-know-something-you-don't-know smile and led me down the hall. My parents were standing in the new room.

225

"Surprise!" they cried. All my things had been arranged in a new maple bedroom suite. My clothes hung in the closet; my Nancy Drew mysteries lined the built-in bookshelf. I was overwhelmed.

"Daddy knew you needed your own room," my mother said. "So he decided you should have this one."

That night, tucked up in my very own bedroom and staring out the window at the suddenly mysterious and alien back yard in the darkness, I experienced a strange emotion. I was lonely. I had Nancy Drew for company, but I missed my sister's sleepy mumbles. "If you don't turn that flashlight off, I'm telling Mom" had somehow become a missed comfort rather than an annoying threat.

I tiptoed to Linda's room. She was still awake. Together, we tiptoed back to the new room, turned off the lights and huddled under the covers, giggling. We told each other ghost stories, each begging the other halfway through to stop. Beyond the long windows, moonlight sifted through the branches of the maple tree.

"I'm glad you're back here," Linda said.

I was touched. "Really?"

"Uh-huh. Because now I've finally got a room of my own."

Making the decision to have a child—it's
momentous. It is to decide forever to have your
heart go walking around outside your body.

ELIZABETH STONE

RACE FOR LOVE

BY

KEITH J. LEENHOUTS

One hundred and forty high school runners fidgeted nervously at the starting line, anxiety momentarily aging their young faces, as they contemplated the grueling three-mile cross-country race that lay ahead. All were dedicated athletes who had run between five and fifteen miles every day for most of their high-school years to prepare themselves for this climactic race, the Michigan High School Cross Country Championship.

For one of the runners, a tall, spindly, awkward-looking boy named Bill, the significance of this race reached far beyond the pursuit of athletic victory. For Bill, our son, it was the most important battle in his eighteen years of struggle against failure. This was Bill's last race. Would it end in a long-awaited victory of the heart—or in a final, crushing defeat of his spirit?

Bill looked pale and nervous as the runners took their places at the line. I wondered if he really belonged here. Certainly most of the other runners were endowed with greater strength and speed. But nobody had ever invented a scale to assess the strength of a young man's heart, or the limits of his desire. Could Bill's inner qualities carry him to his dream of being an "all-state" runner? He would have to finish in the top 15 to earn that honor.

It seemed impossible. In theory, by comparing his qualifying time with the times of the other runners, he should finish close to last. And so another defeat seemed inevitable.

In his 18 years, Bill had already suffered more than his share of set-backs and ridicule. Grade school had been a long nightmare for him. Though he tried very hard, six-year-old Bill could not seem to grasp reading fundamentals. When it was decided that he should repeat first grade, he didn't complain; he simply tried harder. But he still was unable to learn at the same pace as his younger classmates, who added to his burden by constantly mocking him for "flunking."

Then, when he was only nine, his third-grade teacher called my wife and me into her office for a special conference. We approached it with fear and concern. Had Bill misbehaved? Wasn't he trying?

Bill's teacher came directly to the point. "I'm afraid I have some unpleasant news for you," she said. "Your son will never be able to attend college. He tries hard, but he just doesn't have the mental ability."

I leaned back in my chair, breathed deeply, and then said, "Oh, is that all? We were afraid you had some really bad news."

Her concerned expression turned to one of bewilderment. "Isn't it important to you that your son go to college?" she asked. "Don't you feel he *must?* After all, you are a judge. What will people think if the judge's son doesn't go to college?"

I explained that we certainly hoped Bill could go to college someday, but that it was more important for us that he grow up with a love for the Lord and his fellow man, and with the desire to always do his best.

Bill continued to struggle along desperately. But then, in the sixth grade, another teacher called us in for a conference. "I'm sorry to tell you this," she said. "But Bill isn't trying anymore—he has given up completely."

I was saddened by her words. And I was afraid—afraid that Bill might have lost forever a good feeling about himself, that precious but fragile self-image that alone could tip the balance away from failure in later years.

At bedtime I told him, for the first time, about my own grade-school experiences, how some 30 years before I had been the dumbest kid in the class but that, with some love and understanding from my parents and teachers, I had somehow stumbled through those years and had ultimately gone on to law school. I also told him that it was easy to conclude that the achievements of others came simply and easily, but that life was not usually like that. Most triumphs grow out of the ashes of defeat. "Bill," I concluded, "I know that someday, in some way, you will overcome your defeats."

"You know, Dad," he replied, "I guess that not doing so good isn't all that bad if someone loves you and stands by you."

Crack! The starter's gun signaled the beginning of the race. My knees were weak, and a voice that sounded distant and husky left my throat on the chill November wind. "Go, Billy Blue!" I shouted to my son, who wore the blue of the Royal Oaks' Kimbal High School.

I hurried with the rest of the crowd to a flat stretch at the bottom of the hill where we could next see the runners, reaching it just as the first boy burst into view. Though I couldn't see his face, I could tell by his style that it wasn't Bill.

Four more runners appeared, then five. Where was he? For a moment I was struck by a sickening thought that perhaps Bill had dropped out. He had never quit a race, no matter how badly he was running, but there was always a chance of stomach cramps or a sprain.

Finally, he came over the brow of the hill, very erect, his right shoulder lurching up and down with each pumping motion of his loosely swinging arms. The stride was unmistakable. But my heart sank, for there were 39 runners ahead of him. And I could tell that Bill was working hard—too hard. Every muscle was forcing and straining.

But suddenly Bill moved to the outside and began to pass some runners. He knew, and so did I, that he could not afford to fall very far behind, for he did not have a "kick," a burst of speed, that he could rely on at the end of the race. As he swept by me, he raised his right fist just a little. "Go, Blue," I yelled to encourage all the Royal Oak's runners. But deep in my heart I knew who Blue was; it was "Billy Blue."

Our son's puzzling academic problems were finally traced to a paralyzed muscle in one eye, which caused him to suffer occasional double vision and severe perceptual difficulties. As junior high approached, Bill began to work with an eye doctor who developed exercises to help his perception and coordination, and with a special reading tutor. And, through sheer desire, he began to make progress. In fact, to everyone's amazement, he made the honor roll in his first year of junior high.

That spring, Bill tried out for the junior-high baseball team. His attempts at sports were every bit as bad as his early performance in school, though he worked hard and never missed a practice. But winning was such an important consideration that the coach let Bill play in only two games and didn't let him bat—not once—all year.

Bill decided that he didn't care to try out again for a sport where so much emphasis was placed on winning, where no matter how hard he worked, he probably wouldn't get to play. So, in the eighth grade, he went out for track, a sport where no one was ever cut from the team.

During his first track season, Bill lost every race badly. But with every defeat he grew more determined. The next fall, he ran with the high school freshmen cross-country team. He finished poorly all year, but always ran as hard as he could. The team captain and top runner,

We never know the love of the parent until we become parents ourselves.

HENRY WARD BEECHER

231

Phil Ceeley, took notice of his determination and began helping him. And now our son became a familiar figure on Royal Oak's streets, running up to 15 miles a day—everyday—through the snow, sleet and bitter cold of winter, and the sultry heat of the summer.

Those thousands of miles of hard work finally began to pay off in Bill's senior year. He became his cross-country team's fastest runner, and his teammates selected him as one of their co-captains. Yet his goal of being all-state still seemed unobtainable. To achieve it, he would have to beat literally thousands of runners, most with more natural ability than he, in a regional and finally a state meet. "And that," I thought to myself, "is impossible."

The gently rolling hills had now become a torturous ordeal for the runners, and I wondered what force drove each of them on. Surely some of them ran for status and prestige. Would this sustain them more than love and desire? Would the love my wife and I had for Bill, and our efforts to make him feel proud of himself, help him to do something he might not be able to do all by himself?

I ran with the other spectators to the three-quarter-mile mark, where we would next see the runners. There the rolling hills were abruptly interrupted by a dense forest pierced only by a small foot trail. Gasping for breath out of excitement and exertion, I leaned against the trunk of an aging pine—and waited.

A lone runner burst over the crest of the hill—not Bill—and gracefully galloped down the grassy slope. Then a swarm of skinny, red-faced boys appeared. Ten . . . 13 . . . 16 . . . 19 . . . *There he was!* My heart sank. He was running in twentieth place, and pinned to the inside. "You've got to make your move now! You can't do it later," I thought. As if he had heard me, Bill suddenly swung to the outside and spurted from twentieth place to sixth place in less than one hundred yards.

"Go, Ba-ee," I yelled as he streaked past. "Ba-ee"—our sentimental nickname for Bill—had slipped out. When his younger brothers, Dave and Jim, had first started talking, "Ba-ee" was the closest they could come to "Billy." Over the years, we had used "Ba-ee" to tease Bill. But never outside of our home.

My elation suddenly turned to fear as he headed for the trees. He had more than two miles to go. Had he used up too much energy? I knew I would not see him again for about five minutes, while he ran through the woods. I could only wait, worry and wonder.

He came out of the trees at the two-mile mark in a virtual tie for fourth place with a boy who had beaten him badly all year. My heart jumped into my throat—fourth place, even fifth place—either was good enough for all-state! Pain, anxiety and intense desire contorted Bill's slender face. I had never seen him look so strained, so physically and emotionally spent. "Go, Blue! Come on, Ba-ee." Could he hear? Could he feel my love reaching out?

As I rushed past the two-mile mark, I passed close to the finish line, where my wife stood waiting, hoping. "He's fourth," I choked, and turned quickly away as I felt tears welling.

Gasping for breath, I reached the finishing chute, two long ropes that narrowed to a "v" at the finish line. I had just got there when a smooth, confident runner from Grosse Pointe crossed the finish line to the cheers of the spectators. Then the second and third runners streaked down the chute. An eternity later came Bill, still matching his competitor stride for stumbling stride.

Both of the exhausted runners crossed the finish line together. I looked closely at Bill's face. Agony twisted his boyish features as he staggered aimlessly on. Thinking he was about to collapse, I instinctively ducked under the ropes, ran over, grabbed his arm and put it over my shoulder. He rasped and gasped uncontrollably for breath as he slumped lifelessly against me. In a few seconds he straightened up. "I'm okay now, Dad," he said. And he jogged off to "warm down." He had recovered.

But I had not. I was overwhelmed. I tried to hold back the tears that welled in my eyes, but couldn't. I had to let them come. I tried to look at Bill, but could not see. I tried to talk, but no words came.

For a moment I was ashamed. The everyday mask we all wear had been shattered unexpectedly, and I wondered what others would think. But deep in my heart I knew that I wept in a manner that made weeping appropriate; yes, one might even say, majestic.

Children are the living messages we send

to a time we will not see.

JOHN W. WHITEHEAD

ROCKY

BY

MAX APPLE

When I returned from my honeymoon, the woman watching the dog, George, refused to give the pooch back because her kids wanted to keep him.

"Nobody can take what's not theirs," my grandfather Rocky told me and my bride, Debby, firmly. "That's what the Communists do."

The three of us went to the woman's house, and she promptly warned us that the cops were on their way. Then she saw Rocky—all five feet of him. "Who are you?" she asked.

"Never mind," Rocky replied. "The dog is theirs." My grandfather was ninety-five at the time, but he grabbed the screen door and pulled it out of the molding. George came flying from the house, barking joyfully. "Cheap labor," Rocky said as he examined the damage. "She probably put it in herself."

When the police officer arrived, he led our black mutt to his car, saying, "All I want to know is who the dog belongs to." He then directed the woman to stand at her door and sent Debby across the street. "Now both of you call him."

Debby's plaintive wails were drowned out by the children. George perked up his ears, and then, stopping first to raise his leg against a tree, ran straight to Rocky. Turning to the officer, my grandfather reached into his pocket. "Here's a ten spot so she can fix her door and buy her kids a dog."

Rocky Goodstein was the family pioneer. He'd come to America on his own in 1914 and begun working at a bakery. His Yiddish name was Yerachmiel, but an immigration clerk wrote down Herman. The men at the bakery called him Rocky and the name stuck.

He worked sixteen-hour days so he could bring his wife and two children over from Lithuania. They settled in Grand Rapids, Michigan. When I was growing up, my grandfather let me watch him bake cakes. "Cakes aren't like doughnuts or cookies," he'd explain. "You gotta know what you are doing when you bake cakes." He made doughnuts when he had to, but he hated it. "It's not baking, it's frying," he'd say. Rocky drew the line at the cookies, even at home. "You want cookies, ask Betty Crocker."

My grandparents, parents, sisters and I lived in the same house, and I often slept in Rocky's bedroom. Yet my bond with him began before I was born. Five years earlier, his only son, Max, had died in a car accident. Rocky never mentioned him. What I know of my uncle Max comes from my grandmother, who never stopped mourning him, and from my mother, who even years later visited the cemetery so regularly that tombstones with Hebrew lettering are my earliest memories. In many families there's a single event that changes everything—this was ours. When I was born, I was named after Max, and Rocky looked out for me the rest of his life.

From the start, Rocky had big plans. He wanted me to become a rabbi, so he took me to bearded old men and itinerant young teachers. "Do something," he'd say. "He's growing up like a *goy*." They tried to help me translate Hebrew prayers, but all I could think about was baseball.

Rocky gave up on my intellect, but he had an alternative plan. "You can be a professional man," he said. "You'll never have to work nights." He

talked a pharmacist into letting me help out. I wiped the soda fountain and swept the floors. One day the pharmacist caught me reading a 3-D comic book, and kicked me out. Rocky rubbed my back until I stopped crying, then blamed it all on the pharmacist. After that, we filled prescriptions at the cut-rate store on the other side of town.

Rocky didn't always see things my way, however. When I started playing poker in high school, he threatened to tell the principal. But by then, I had learned how to handle my grandfather. I began putting ten percent of my winnings into his cap—even when I lost.

"You always win?" he finally asked.

"Most of the time. If I don't have the cards, I fold."

"So it's not like you're gambling."

"It's more like investing. If I concentrate, it's like—a job."

I'd said the magic word. He kept his ten percent. When I graduated from high school, he unwrapped his handkerchief of my poker money and bought me a watch.

Rocky began to outlive his town and his time while I was away at college. His wife and friends had passed away, so he was more than happy to share an apartment with me when I went to graduate school in Ann Arbor. At ninety-three, his body seemed to have reached a certain point in aging and then gone on hold. He didn't remain young; he was more like a permanent seventy.

Still it wasn't always easy having your grandfather for a roommate—especially when I first met Debby. "You bring a girl to your apartment without marrying her?" he demanded. "You're lucky I don't call the police."

Later when I married Debby and got a teaching job in Houston, Rocky again came along. My widowed mother, Rocky's daughter, was also ready for a new start. She moved into a house with Rocky two blocks from Debby and me.

My grandfather showed no signs of slowing down. He'd put out his garbage at six A.M., then walk over to do ours. He baked our breads, polished our shoes, and still wanted a hard job—like mowing the lawn. I couldn't let an old man do that in the Houston heat, but I let him sneak in a few minutes when I went inside for water. He'd grab the handle and push at a run until I returned. I'd pretend to be angry, and he would sulk. Then he's point out the spots I had missed.

Rocky never wanted to stay indoors for long, but the birth of our daughter, Jessica, changed that. He'd lie on the floor and let her explore his face, his tie, his polished shoes. Watching her climb all over Rocky, I realized how it must have been for me when I was a baby. He was a living playground.

When Rocky turned ninety-seven, doctors discovered a malignant tumor in his colon. Before operating, the surgeon looked grim—but when everything went well, he changed his mind about Rocky. "He should have been dead twenty years ago," the doctor told me. "I wouldn't bet against this guy."

Two weeks later, Rocky was back putting out our garbage by eight A.M. Still, I worried. "He used to have it out by six," I told Debby.

"He's entitled to slow down," she replied. Debby was right. Rocky had lived to become the favorite playmate of Jessica and, now, Sam. He had lived to see me established in a career, had overcome cancer and cataracts and thirty years of forced retirement and still had the energy to study the Talmud and go to the synagogue every day. When I jogged, I sometimes prayed for him and for a painless end. As it turned out, I should have prayed for someone else.

Debby was struck with multiple sclerosis. It started out with double vision. Then section by section, her body gradually deceived her. She lost feeling in part of a toe, in the bottom of her left foot, in the side of her face. There was no pattern. Some losses were fleeting, some stayed.

Rocky didn't know what to do as Debby's disease progressed. He couldn't understand what was happening. He had lived his century in the world of absolutes. If you were sick, you recovered or you died.

Sam was three, and he couldn't understand either. When Debby was propped up on pillows, he thought she was waiting to read him a story. One night, Sam escaped from his bath towel and jumped on Debby's bed before I could stop him. Her face turned pale; the pouncing on the bed was causing an almost unbearable dizziness. I grabbed my son, put him in his room and shut the door.

"All he wants is a story," Rocky said.

"He'll get it when I have time."

"You never have time for anything anymore," Rocky replied. "Pay attention to your children." He tried to push me away from the door, but I didn't budge. Sam pounced on it. "Let the boy come to me," Rocky said.

I took my hand from the knob. Sam ran right to his great-grandfather and climbed into his arms. Rocky carried him to the living room couch and put him on his lap. Jessica sat beside them. "I'll tell you a story," Rocky began, "about the bakery when I first came to America."

Where Debby's illness was concerned, I divided the world into those who could understand what was happening and those who couldn't. I lumped Rocky into that second group, but he didn't stay there long. One day a nurse at the hospital called. "We're having a problem with Mr. Goodstein," she said. "He wants to give a pint of blood for your wife. We really can't let him at his age."

When I arrived at the blood bank, Rocky was standing at the door as if he expected his number to be called any second. "How can blood be too old?" he asked me. "If it still works, it's good."

"They're not gonna take any from you," I said. "Let's go."

Wisdom is with the aged, and understanding in length of days.

JOB 12

"If you don't want people to give blood," Rocky yelled as we left, "don't say you do on television!"

When Debby's condition deteriorated, she was moved to the hospital, and I visited her every night after work. Rocky, at one-hundred-and-three, bounced into action. He played speedcars with Jessica and Sam, or watched cartoons with them. He supervised at the playground and accompanied me to parent-teacher conferences. He was too busy to die.

For three years Debby fought the good fight, but then the disease overwhelmed her and she steadily worsened. After leaving the hospital one day, I sat outside our house trying to contemplate life without my wife. Rocky came out carrying a cup of ginger ale, his version of medicine. "I'm okay," I told him.

"Drink it anyway," he said. "You'll be more okay."

As soon as I opened the door to come inside, I smelled the aroma. Nine-year-old Jessica was standing on a chair, holding a cookie cutter and licking batter from her fingers. "Do you believe it?" she said. "Rocky's helping me bake cookies!"

The erstwhile cake man had flour up to his elbows—and sheets of cookies on the counter. "We'll have enough for a bake sale," Jessica said.

Jessica and Rocky carried a table to the curb and spread out the cookies. I bought one each from Jessica and Sam. Though the bitterness at the back of my throat didn't leave then or for a long time after (Debby died nine years later), on that day I still could taste the sweetness.

Rocky continued to be a symbol of survival. When he was 106, I was invited to lecture in Brazil. As always, I brought up a difficult subject with Rocky indirectly. "If I go to Brazil," I asked loudly, considering his growing deafness, "can I get you anything?"

I waited for the look in his eyes, his false bravado, his impatience—signs I'd been reading all my life. Only then would I know if my old roommate could give me up for two weeks.

"Maybe you can find me a pair of yellow shoes," he said. "Look around."

I brought back some bright yellow canvas shoes, and Rocky wore them proudly to the synagogue. Before he went into the hospital a few months later, he stuffed them with newspaper and put them in his closet. This time his body was truly failing. His mind was fine, though. "Don't forget," he told me at the hospital. "On Tuesday put out the garbage."

When my mother took the children for some ice cream, Rocky motioned for me to lower his bed. I leaned over the guardrail and yelled in words the maxim he had taught me with his life. *"Shtark zich!"* ("Strengthen yourself!")

He shook his head, and I put my ear close to hear his whisper. *"Ich ken shein nicht."* ("I can't anymore.")

He was sleeping when my mother and the children returned. Jessica had made a discovery in the cafeteria. "Rocky is more than half as old as America!" She showed me her figures on a napkin: 1982 - 1776 = 206. I was still thinking about it back home when my mother called. Rocky was going fast. I got to his room just seconds after he died.

We buried him in Houston, and after I poured the symbolic Texas soil onto the coffin, I laid down the shovel and stepped forward to fulfill the role I'd been born to do—say the Kaddish, the mourner's prayer.

The rabbi held out a book, but I shook my head. I knew the words by heart, yet I began sobbing too much to say them. Rocky didn't like mistakes, and I wanted to get the words right. *"Yisgadal, v'yisgadesh,"* I finally said, almost in a whisper.

As Jessica and Sam watched through tears, I took a deep breath and looked up past the tombstones. *"Shtark zich!"* I told myself—and I did. My voice steadied, and I made no mistakes. By the last stanza, everyone could hear.

Grandchildren are the crown of
the aged.

PROVERBS 17

ACKNOWLEDGMENTS

All the stories in *A Message of Family* previously appeared in *Reader's Digest* magazine. We would like to thank the following contributors and publishers for permission to reprint material.

The Day I Met My Mother by Faith L. Mahaney. © 1981 by Faith L. Mahaney. Escondido Times Advocate (May 10, '81).

"Keep Pedaling, Karen!" by Christopher de Vinck. "ONLY THE HEART KNOWS HOW TO FIND THEM" copyright © 1991 by Christopher de Vinck. Published by Viking Penguin, a division of Penguin Putnam Books USA Inc.

Outside Looking In by Mary Potter. © 1989 by Mary Potter. The Berkshire Eagle (October 3, '89).

My Uncle and Me by Pat Jordan. © 1998 by Pat Jordan. Florida Magazine (May '98).

Sisters Three by Faith Andrews Bedford. From the April 1997 issue of <u>Country Living</u>, © 1997 reprinted by permission of the Hearst Corporation.

The Little China Chip by Bettie B. Youngs. "VALUES FROM THE HEARTLAND: STORIES OF AN AMERICAN FARMGIRL," copyright © 1995 by Bettie B. Youngs. Published by Health Communications, Inc.

A Houseful of Love and Laughter by Jay Leno. "LEADING WITH MY CHIN" copyright © 1996 by Big Dog Productions, Inc. Published by HarperCollins Publishers, Inc.

Surrounded by Brothers by James Schembari. © 1995 by New York Times Co. The New York Times (December 14, '95).

Why I Wear a Plastic Dinosaur by Dan Schaeffer. © 1993 by Pastor Dan Schaeffer. Pursuit (December '93).

Stories on a Headboard by Elaine Pondant. © 1993 by Elaine Pondant. Home Life (August '93).

Quotations

Photo Credits

Cover: Michele Salmieri/FPG; Title page: Ross Whitaker/Image Bank; p. 2-3: Photodisc; p. 5: Gilles Larrain/Graphistock; p. 5-6: Photodisc; p. 9: Amy Guip/Graphistock; p. 10-11: Stephen Simson/FPG; p. 13: Rosanne Olson/Graphistock; p. 14: Photodisc; p. 16: Photodisc; p. 20-21: Zephyr; p. 22-23: Ostentoshi & Zoda/Envision; p. 25: Larry Maglott/Image Bank; p. 28-29: Photodisc; p. 31: J. P. Williams/Stone; p. 32-33: Photodisc; p. 37: Keith Gunner/Weststock; p. 40-41: Photodisc; p. 42: Janet Beller/Graphistock; p. 46: David Falconer/Weststock; p. 48-49: Peter Johansky/Envision; p. 51: Photodisc; p. 52-53: Adam Jones/Photo Researchers; p. 56: Steve Needham/Envision; p. 58-59: Photodisc; p. 61: Felicia Martinez/Photoedit; p. 64-65: Photodisc; p. 66: Julie Habel/Corbis; p. 71: Telegraph Colour Library/FPG; p. 72-73: Telegraph Colour Library/FPG; p. 74: Don Wilson/Weststock; p. 76-77: Photodisc; p. 80: Photodisc; p. 84-85: Jerald Frampton/Graphistock; p. 87: Photodisc; p. 88-89: Tom Francisco/Graphistock; p. 91: Photodisc; p. 94-95: Susie Cusher/Graphistock; p. 97: Ken Redding/Corbis; p. 98-104: Photodisc; p. 136: Telegraph Colour Library/FPG; p. 138-39: Dan Goode/Photo Researchers; p. 140: John Williams/Bruce Coleman; p. 142-43: Photodisc; p. 145: Photodisc; p. 148-49: Johner Bildburg/Photonica; p. 152: Photodisc; p. 156-57: Jerry Gay/Stone; p. 159: Steve Needham/Envision; p. 163: Lars Topelman/Graphistock; p. 164-65: Photodisc; p. 167: Julie Habel/Corbis; p. 168-69: Ed Holub/Photonica; p. 171: M. Tokunaga/Photonica; p. 174-75: Jill Greenburg/Graphistock; p. 177-87: Photodisc; p. 190-91: Carol Lee/Weststock; p. 192-93: Photodisc; p. 194: Photodisc; p. 199: Noel Reichel/FPG; p. 200-207: Photodisc; p. 209: BDR Associates/Corbis; p. 210-11: Patricia Heal/Graphistock; p. 212: H. Horenstein/Photonica; p. 217: Zephyr; p. 218-19: Renee Demartin/Weststock; p. 221: Knudson Photography/Weststock; p. 224-25: Photodisc; p. 227: Howard Schatz/Graphistock; p. 228-29: Zephyr; p. 232: Gary Wade/Stone; p. 235: Zephyr; p. 236-37: Photodisc; p. 239: Photodisc; p. 243: Zephyr

Carousel Research: Laurie Platt Winfrey, Van Bucher, Cristian Pena, Peter Tomlinson